Queenpins

NOTORIOUS WOMEN GANGSTERS OF THE MODERN ERA

STRATEGIC MEDIA BOOKS, LLC
ROCK HILL, SOUTH CAROLINA, AND THUNDER
BAY, CANADA

For Magdalena, my wife, my inspiration and love of my life
—Ron Chepesiuk

TABLE OF CONTENTS

The cut throat world of organized crime has long been dominated by men, and such macho godfathers and kingpins as Al Capone, John Dillinger, Pablo Escobar and John Gotti have become legendary. Yet, dig deep into the annals of crime and one can find smart, ambitious and ruthless women who have cracked the glass ceiling of the underworld and became notorious in their own right. Little has been written about these queenpins; that is, until now. For the first time, I profile the major queenpins of modern times and how they not only survived but thrived in gangland.

Queenpins: The Lives and Times of Notorious Women Gangsters provides an engrossing and fresh look at life in the highest echelons of the criminal world. Some of these queen-pins have become well-known, thanks to Hollywood and the ubiquitous media. Others are not so well known. Many rose and fell in the world of drug trafficking. Others achieved notoriety as madams, bank robbers, bootleggers, and gambling. Several operated in the U.S., but there are queenpins in China, Colombia, Mexico, Australia, Italy and even India whose stories chronicled.

"Queenpins" offers a fresh but engrossing look at crime history. You will discover Stephanie St. Clair who got rich in the numbers game and then became a legend when she stood up to mobster Dutch Shultz, who wanted to put her out of business. In the 1920s, Gertrude Lythgoe was known as the "Queen of the Bahamas" for her bootlegging exploits. Gertrude's nickname was "Cleo" because people thought her exotic looks made her a dead ringer for Queen Cleopatra. Kathryn Kelly was the master of public relations and marketing who turned her unambitious husband, Machine Gun Kelly, into one of the FBI's most targeted criminals. Griselda Blanco, the so-called Black Widow, taught infamous drug lord Pablo Escobar the tricks of the cocaine trade and sparked a crime wave in Miami that left hundreds dead. Xie Caiping, the Mama San of Chinese crime, led a shocking life of decadence, excess and sexual depravity while dominating the Shanghai underworld. Sandra Beltran Avila, the Queen of the Pacific was beautiful and vain, but she skillfully used her assets to build powerful alliances between Colombian and Mexican drug cartels, an accomplishment that fueled the Latin American drug trade.

The stories of these queenpins need to be told; their place in crime history, documented. My research reveals the important role that women have played and can play in organized crime. I hope to inform and I hope you enjoy.

The Best Madam in America

I N 1912, PEARL Adler, a 12-year old girl from the small village of Yanow, Russia, embarked on a long, perilous oceanic journey. For support, the young girl, whom her family called "Polly," had nothing more with her than the high expectations of her large family and a potato sack that contained her belongings, some garlic, apples, four loaves of black bread and four hunks of salami that her mother Gertrude had packed for her. Joining Polly on board the good ship Naftar was a diverse mix of Poles, Italians, Danes and Swedes, all determined to make a prosperous new life for themselves in the Promised Land of America. It was a rough voyage and nearly all the passengers got sick, but not Polly. No sickness was going to impede her determination to reach America.

Unlike many of her fellow passengers, Polly did not leave a life of abject poverty. She was the eldest child in a family that included two daughters and seven sons. But her father, Morris Adler, was a tailor, a respectable occupation, and the family was well-off by Yanow standards. Still, the family's ethnic roots were Jewish and it was a time of virulent anti Semitism in Russia. The Adler family could be a victim of a pogrom, or violent attack, at any time. It had happened frequently between 1903 and 1905.

In the course of one week alone, there had been fifty anti-Jewish pogroms. In the village of Binlystok, for instance, 19 Jews were murdered and 24 injured. The Kishinew pogrom left 120 dead and 500 injured, while the Odessa pogrom had 299 victims.

Until the pogroms, Morris Adler's plan for Polly was to have her attend school in a nearby village and then complete her education under the village Rabbi's guidance. Given the insecurities of life in Russia, the father decided that she would be the first link in a line of emigration that would bring his family to America.

The voyage was Polly's first taste of freedom from the strictures of rural life and she was wired with excitement and anticipation. When the day of arrival finally a came and the ship glided into New York City harbor, Polly joined her fellow passengers on deck.

A male passenger shouted in Yiddish: "The American Lady: The Statue of Liberty!"

The passengers gazed and marveled. Polly joined in a chorus of ecstatic shouts and screams. After de-embarking, Polly caught the train to Holyoke, Massachusetts, where the Grodesky family claimed her at the depot. The Grodeskys were not friends of the Adlers, but friends of friends, and they had agreed to take care of Polly, provided the Adlers paid for her upkeep and schooling.

Polly arrived two years before the start of World War I, but the war's outbreak cut off communication with her family and the money it provided for her, dashing the family's hope of joining their daughter in the New World. It was a bad break, one of many Polly would have before eventually finding success in her new life. Eventually, she would make money, enjoy a comfortable lifestyle and mix with the rich and powerful. As a leading member of world's so called oldest profession, Polly

Polly Adler

would claim as her friends not only members of New York's elite but also some of the most prominent gangsters of her time, bringing her more notoriety than admiration. **POLLY'S FIRST JOB** hardly fit her vision of the American Dream. With World War I in full swing, cut off from money from home and on her own, Polly had to find a job to pay for her keep. She found one at a paper factory, a sweat shop that paid her three dollars a week. Two years later, her father decided to send Polly to Brooklyn, New York, to live with her cousins, the Rosen family. The change was a shock to Polly. As she later explained: "The Grodeskys had not been rich, but compared to the Rosens their house was the Taj Mahal."

Polly found another job in a corset factory, making five dollars a week, from which she had to pay three dollars for room and board and a $1.20 for car fare and lunches. Polly hungered for an education, and she continued to attend night school as time from her job allowed, hoping once again to get on the path to the American Dream. Money was tight and Polly had to walk a mile to and from school so she could pay for her lunches.

By 1917 the factory had closed down, but in April of that year, the U.S. entered the Great War and Polly found another job at a factory manufacturing soldier's shirts. At age 17, she stood just 4' 11" tall and had matured physically. A new foreman at the factory named Frank noticed her. Young and naïve, Polly loved the attention. Frank invited her to go to Coney Island on a date and Polly eagerly accepted. The date turned into a nightmare. Instead of going to Coney Island, Frank took her to a cottage where they were alone. He tried seducing Polly, but put off by his rough advances, Polly got scared and resisted. Frank knocked her out cold and raped her.

A month went by at the factory as if nothing had happened. Polly was ashamed and afraid. Then Polly discovered she was pregnant. Sidonia, a friend and worker at the factory, took Polly to a doctor to see about an abortion. It cost $150 but all Polly had in savings was $35. Polly went to Frank but he refused to help. Sidonia found a doctor who was willing to perform the abortion for $35. When the doctor heard Polly's sad story, he took just $25 for his fee and told her to use the other $10 to buy shoes and stockings. The experience traumatized the young girl.

"I went through the motions of living," Polly Adler later recalled. "I was changed; I had lost heart. I no longer had hope."

Polly's fortunes continued to decline. Frank harassed her at work and she quit her job. She met Harry Richman, a performer who later became a Broadway star, and they became friends. Harry invited Polly to a nightclub, where, for the first time in her life, she drank something stronger than soda pop. She gulped the whiskey as it was soft drink. Blind drunk and out all night, her clothes disheveled, Polly was a mess when she got back to her home in Brooklyn. The Rosens did not like what they saw and kicked Polly out of the house, telling her to leave immediately. Polly quickly wrapped her clothes in a newspaper and left.

In her autobiography, *A House is not a Home*, Polly summed up her life in America to this point: "So far I had certainly racked up a row of goose eggs in the Golden Land. I had failed in my quest for an education. I might have gotten back home. I had lost my virginity, my reputation and my job. All I had gotten was older."

POLLY FOUND A cheap, $20 a month, windowless apartment at Second Avenue and North Street and began hunting for a job. She spent two tough weeks looking, hungry and frustrated, before finding another dreary, dead-end and low-paying factory job. She worked at it for about a year before bumping into a fellow Russian Jew named Abe Shornik, a man about Polly's father's age who worked in a dress factory. He was a gentleman who took an interest in Polly's welfare, introducing her to a well-to-do dress manufacturer in the hope that he would hire her.

The dress manufacturer was related to the head of a big theatrical supply house, and Polly was introduced to the theater crowd. Polly became friends with a beautiful blond actress and singer whom she identified as Joan Smith. The actress brought Polly over to her apartment and introduced her to several of her friends in show business. A brand new world opened for the young girl and Polly loved it. About a month after they met, Joan invited Polly to move in with her at her nice apartment on Riverside Drive.

Polly lived with Joan through the spring of 1920, but then Joan began to change. The heroin and cocaine she used in abundance made her frequently temperamental, often sullen and sometimes violent. Joan behavior concerned Polly, but when Joan started showing tender feelings towards her, Polly knew it was time to leave. She became friends with a bookkeeper she identified as Tony and confided her troubles. Tony offered the use of his apartment, provided Polly help him out. He would pay the rent if Polly allowed him to meet a lady friend at the pad. Not really considering the implications of the offer and desperate to get out her dead end life, Polly jumped at it, and with the money Tony gave her, rented a two-room furnished apartment on Riverside.

Tony's affair did not last long, and a few weeks after she had moved into the apartment, Tony asked Polly to find him another woman. He would pay Polly $50 and the woman she provided, $100. Polly accepted and found Tony a pretty blonde. Polly was now in a new line of work.

"It was in this informal, almost casual fashion that I began my career as a madam," Polly wrote in her autobiography. "I didn't think of it then as a career or myself as a madam. I suppose, in the way, people do, I managed to sell myself a bill of goods—I didn't invent sex. Nobody had to come to my apartment who didn't want to. I was really doing them a favor—that sort of thing."

BUT POLLY HAD found her calling and her life changed dramatically. She bought nice clothes and frequented speakeasies and dance halls. She met several wealthy men, and to those whom she believed would be discrete, she gave her address. Polly hired three girls which began entertaining her acquaintances several times a week. Polly had no illusions about her new found career. After tasting the good life and making good money, it was a question for her of economics, not morals. No way did she want to go back to her former lifestyle that left her wondering from where her next dollar would come.

It wasn't too long, though, before Polly was booked on suspicion of prostitution. It would be the first of seventeen such arrests in her long sex industry career. The case, like the many others that followed during Polly's life as a madam, was dismissed because of a lack of evidence.

Polly moved ahead in her new profession with the energy and smarts of an entrepreneur, even though it was not an easy profession in which to succeed. Prostitution's illegality made the consequences of arrest very serious. By 1917, the anti prostitution efforts of the so-called Progressive Era had closed down every important red light district in the U.S., including the hitherto untouchable Storyville in New Orleans. The following year, prostitution was illegal in nearly every state in the Union. One of the biggest brothels in America, the Speedway Inn, was run by the notorious gangster Al "Scarface" Capone of Chicago. Capone and the criminal underworld took over much of the sex trade, and gangsters were not inclined to treat women of the night decently.

Polly was trying to run a high class house of ill repute, but she had to pay protection money to the gangsters. It was an experience shared by other madams of the day.

Helen McGowan, a Detroit madam, recalled what it was like being a madam in the 1920s: "If the take was a thousand dollars for a particular night, five hundred went to the racket boys, four hundred to the girls and $100 to me. The great bulk of our funds went to hoodlums and lawyers, thanks to our righteous laws that protect the public against the world's oldest profession."

Polly did not have problems with the criminal element, and she began building her clientele in a discrete business like manner. At the night clubs Polly patronized, she advised head-waiters and captains that her establishment was not your typical whorehouse, and they should only send men to her bordello who could afford to pay $20 or more. For those who could pay that amount, Polly Adler was available 24 hours a day. The money began rolling in, and by the spring of 1921 she had saved $6,000.

In her mind, Polly thought her career choice would only be temporary until she found success in a legitimate business. Polly saw an opportunity and she and a friend opened a lingerie shop at 2487 Broadway. The business broke even at first, but, unfortunately for Polly, she and her partner were inexperienced business-wise and they had no cash in reserve to cover the lean times a start up can experience. Meanwhile, their business became prey to crafty shoplifters who stole the owners blind. The business closed after a year.

Once again, Polly was broke. Her total assets consisted of her furniture, a dog named Nicko and $800 in cash. Her financial situation continued to deteriorate, and when she was down to her last $100, Polly once again entered the prostitution business. This time it would be for good; however, her clientele was different. Many her new clients were gangsters, some of whom would become the country's biggest mobsters of the 1920s and '30s. They were often drunk and unruly. When some of the gangsters roughed up one of her girls, she decided to move, hoping to attract a more civil clientele. To stay ahead of the law, Polly adopted the tactic of moving from apartment to apartment, before eventually settling into a large rented apartment near 7th Avenue.

SHE NOW SET out to be, in her paraphrased words, "the best goddamn madam in America." Once again, she exhibited the Midas touch when it came to whoredom. She could now afford the sumptuous style of a successful madam and hired an interior decorator, spending lavishly on furnishings, and carpets, while lining her walls with books. Much of the expensive décor in her bordello was in the style of Louis XV and Louis XVI. She also hired a cook, maid and hairdresser.

In the late 1920s she set up shop at the majestic Tower at 215 West 75th Street, an edifice of the firm of Schwartz and Gross, one of the major designers of hotels and high rise buildings in the early 20th century. In an interview with writer Lisa Jacobs, James Nassy, a long time resident of the Majestic Towers, revealed that the building, with its many hidden stairways and secret door ways, was designed as a bordello.

"The layout was conceived to protect secretive behavior," Nassy explained.

Given her hours of operation and her business success, Adler did not have much of a personal life. She was in her 20s and single but stayed to herself and rarely dated.

Later Polly recalled: "I couldn't behave like other women and the house was forever uppermost in my mind, and it was too much to expect a man to take out a woman who can't keep her mind on the date, who remains a business machine even off duty and even in an ostentatiously hilarious mood. So I decided the best thing I could do was put me as a private citizen in cold storage, and so long as I was madam, 'temporarily disconnect' my life."

Polly's life was her work, and her bordello became a kind of clubhouse where the women were not necessarily the main attraction. Patron from the elite and privileged class began to frequent her bordello, coming as much for the drinks, the socializing and the card games as for the prostitutes. The clientele included members of the famous Algonquin Roundtable, a group of influential New York City intellectuals, journalists, editors, writers and artists that began lunching together at the Algonquin Hotel in June 1919 and continued on a regular basis for the next eight years. In their articles and columns, the journalists in the group disseminated the gist of their conversations across the country.

Algonquin Roundtable members included Robert Benchley, Dorothy Parker, George S. Kauffman and Edna Farber. Benchley was a wit, writer and humorist who wrote essays and articles for *Vanity Fair* and *The New Yorker* magazines. He was also a film director whose movie, "How to Sleep," won in the Best Short Subject category at the 1933 Academy Awards.

Benchley liked to rent Polly's establishment for lavish parties. At one of them, a despondent prostitute jumped out of an open window. Benchley checked to see that she was okay and insisted that the party goers keep celebrating. Polly remembered Benchley fondly, describing him as "one of the kindest, warmest hearted man in the world."

Benchley's friend, Dorothy Parker, a poet and writer, also frequented Polly's bordello. Following the breakup of the Roundtable, Parker traveled to Hollywood to pursue a screenwriting career. She received two Oscar nominations for her work, but as a result of her left wing political activism, was placed on Hollywood's Black List. Both Parker and Benchley helped Polly pick out books for her bordello. Roundtable member George S. Kaufman, who was lauded as Broadway's greatest comic dramatist, reportedly had a charge account with Polly.

Jimmy Walker, another client, was mayor of New York City from 1925 to 1932 when he was charged with corruption and resigned. When Mickey Walker started frequenting Polly's bordello, he was the world's middleweight boxing champion. Naïve about the role of a madam, Walker kept propositioning Polly to go to bed with him. Polly had to take one of Mickey's handlers aside and tell him that she was the madam of the establishment and was not available. Further, if the champ kept badgering her, he would have to leave. Walker got the message, straightened up, and eventually, Polly became fond of him.

IN ADDITION TO the intellectual elite, some of the most notorious gangsters in American history frequented Adler's bordello. The most powerful, no doubt, was Charles "Lucky" Luciano, a Sicilian mobster who by 1925 was grossing more than $300,000 annually from overseeing the Big Apple's largest bootleg operation. In a power struggle within La Cosa Nostra, Luciano outmaneuvered two other prominent mobsters, Joe Masseria and Salvatore Maranzano, to become the most dominant godfather in America. Luciano headed a Mob Commission that oversaw its nationwide activities.

Polly considered Lucky a gentleman and recalled that success did not change him. During their friendship, Lucky remained quiet, polite and considerate of her girls. The feeling was mutual. In his 1962 autobiography, Luciano spoke warmly of Polly, the madam, enthusing that Polly ran "the best damn whorehouse in New York."

In 1936, New York State Special Prosecutor Thomas Dewey, a future Republican presidential candidate, successfully prosecuted Luciano for operating a prostitution ring. Polly expressed amazement that Luciano had been linked to prostitution since she often supplied Luciano with girls when he entertained.

"I think Dewey never called me as witness because the only testimony I could possibly give was in favor of the defense (Luciano)," she later recalled.

Adler's relationship with another prominent gangster, Dutch Schultz, was much more complicated. By the time Polly met Dutch, he was one of the most influential gangsters in New York City. Born Arthur Flegenheimer in 1902, Schultz was known as "The Beer Baron of the Bronx" for his phenomenal success in the illegal bootlegging industry, which made him a fortune and one of the richest gangsters in New York City during Prohibition. In the early to mid 1930s, Dutch took over the Harlem numbers racket after a bitter battle with a queenpin named Stephanie St. Clair and became even richer.

When Polly first met Dutch, she was still trying to recover financially from the Stock Market Crash of 1929. In their initial meeting, Dutch gave Polly a thousand dollars, instructing her to: "Use the money to get a bigger apartment. You will be seeing a lot of me."

With that revelation, Schultz proceeded to Polly's bedroom and fell asleep on her bed. After Adler moved into the new apartment, Dutch used the bedroom to run his criminal business.

Polly later recalled: "I realized this was the first of many nights. By taking Dutch's money, I was on my way out of my financial hole, but in return, I had put myself in bondage—from now on my life will be ruled by fear."

Polly viewed Schultz as a psychopath who could go ballistic at the slightest provocation, and she knew well his reputation for violence. Schultz's henchmen once kidnapped a stubborn wholesale beer distributor named Joe Rock, who had refused to let the Dutchman bully him out of business. The thugs beat Rock, strung him up by his thumbs, and then put a strip of gauze smeared with infectious material across his eyes and taped the gauze securely. By the time they tossed Rock out in the street, the hapless wholesaler was probably blind and crippled by the severe beating. The message was clear: Do not mess with the Dutchman.

Polly would never know when the unpredictable gangster would show up at her apartment. The strain was intense, but she never did get up the nerve to tell Schultz to take his patronage elsewhere.

Polly was also in fear of Dutch's rivals, especially a gangster named Vincent "Mad Dog" Coll. Coll earned his nickname, from the media after he had killed a child in a botched assassination attempt. Coll had been a Schultz enforcer but decided to organize his own gang. The ambitious Mad Dog had tried to kill Dutch, and Polly worried that the gangster might get the wrong idea if he learned Dutch was hanging out at her apartment. Polly's anxiety ended when Schultz had Coll murdered.

Schultz tried to dominate Polly's life. Punctually around 7 at night, the gangster would take a bath, commanding Polly to scrub his back. He once ordered her never to drink, fearing that, if she did, she might get careless and talk too much. But one day Polly returned home inebriated. Schultz got angry and asked her where she had been. He didn't like Polly's answer and decided to teach her a lesson. He punched Polly on top of the head, knocking her to the floor, and stormed out of the apartment.

Terrified, Polly moved to West 54th Street, hoping to break free of the Dutchman, but a few weeks later, he showed up again. He didn't apologize for beating her but gave her $500.

"Next week is Christmas," the gangster said. "Buy yourself a gift."

AS ADLER GREW in prominence in the New York bordello scene, Dutch Schultz was not her biggest worry. Polly's association with major underworld figures had drawn the attention of the authorities. Adler had entertained many members of the court, law enforcement officers and officials in city government agencies, and she had paid thousands of dollars in bribes—half of her income by some estimates—to keep her bordello running smoothly and to keep her call girls out of jail. She had made sure all of her bases were covered. For instance, half of the head waiters in Manhattan were said to be on her payroll.

So Polly was not particularly worried when ex judge Samuel Seabury began conducting an investigation into the New York sex trade in 1929. The Magistrate's Court of the City of New York was the court in which many people charged with crimes first encountered the legal system. Seabury headed the Commission investigating the charges of widespread corruption within the municipal court system as well as the police force. Among the allegations found to be true—hundreds of women had to pay exorbitant bonds or go to prison on dubious convictions for prostitution. Throughout the autumn of 1930, the Seabury Commission heard testimony from more than 1,000 witnesses—judges, lawyers, police officers and former defendants—describe and document the corruption.

Polly did not want to testify, but the Seabury Commission wanted to know why she had never been convicted of prostitution, even though she had been arrested eleven times. Polly's name had come up in the testimony of John C. Weston, a former official in the New York City's District's Attorney's Office. Weston admitted to being bribed twice to "go easy" when Polly appeared before the Magistrate Court judges.

According to a *New York Herald* report: "Weston testified that Adler is represented by lawyers who were in the habit of bribing him to lay down when their client's interests were concerned."

Weston further stated that Polly's power and influence was so great that a prosecutor could be removed unless he "laid down" when prosecuting a charge against her.

Then Polly received a call from an anonymous source warning her to leave the house immediately because representatives of the court were on their way to serve her a subpoena. Polly threw her clothes in a bag, dashed out of her apartment and hailed a cab. Polly headed for Newark, New Jersey, where she checked into a hotel.

Later Adler explained her reasoning for leaving town: "I had to get out of town because I wasn't

Polly Adler being arrested

going to squeal; if I accepted a subpoena, a lot of people might be dubious about my ability to keep clammed up and decide to insure my silence in ways I didn't care to dwell on."

Polly eventually fled to Miami, Florida, where she checked into a hotel under an assumed name. Polly knew she could not be extradited from Florida so long as she stayed out of New York State. Polly was a celebrity—the Big Apple's most famous madam. The New York newspapers reported rumors speculating on where she was hiding. Meanwhile, representatives of thirteen of New York's best known and respected hotels, including the Biltmore, the Ritz, the Carleton and the Vanderbilt, were summoned before the Seabury Commission in the hope they could help the authorities trace Polly's calls.

Eventually, Adler tired of life on the lam. In need of money, she returned to New York City and turned herself in. Surrendering on May 7, 1930, Polly publicly vowed never to tell what she knew about the New York City vice trade. Adler was grilled about her financial affairs and her dealings with an Irwin

O'Brien, a former member of the New York City vice squad. Charges were brought against many corrupt officials, but not because of Adler's testimony. The madam did not wilt under the questioning and denied everything.

Ironically, Polly Adler believed the Seabury Commission investigation actually helped her illicit business. In her memoir, she recalled: "I found when I got back to business that the Seabury investigation has sure as hell made my life easier. The police no longer were a headache; there was no more kowtowing to double crossing Vice Squad men. No more hundred dollar handshakes, no more police raids to up the month's quota. In fact, thanks to Judge Seabury and his not very merry men, I was able to operate three years without breaking a lease."

FOR THE NEXT five years, Polly continued to be one of the country's most successful and high profile madams. Then New York City began another anti corruption campaign under Fiorello LaGuardia, the New York City mayor from 1934 to 1945.

LaGuardia went after Lucky Luciano, Frank Costello and other mob bosses, declaring: "Let's drive the bums out of town." LaGuardia had well known gangsters arrested whenever they appeared in public and waged war against the gambling rackets.

On July 10, 1936, police and city officials knocked down the doors of Adler's sixth floor Central Park West apartment. The officials found Adler, a 25-year old black woman and two men sitting at a table, drinking. Under questioning, the two men revealed that Adler had "procured" two women for them. Adler was arrested and arraigned; bail was set at $1,000. It was Adler's sixteenth arrest in her career as a madam.

"I can't possibly furnish that much," Adler complained to the magistrate. "I'm broke now and I owe a lot. Besides, I'm innocent of this charge."

The case was continuously postponed, but whenever Polly appeared in court, the press would report about her, often with sympathetic observations. *The New York Daily News*, for example, wrote: "The police tap this woman's wires… and in other ways keep her under surveillance as if they suspected her of being the Lindbergh kidnapper."

Polly pled guilty and received a sentence of 30 days in jail and a $500 fine. In her autobiography, Adler claimed that a well-known gangster helped get the charge reduced from what could have been a three-year sentence. She felt lucky to spend only 24 days of her sentence in jail, given that she was at center stage of La Guardia's anti corruption campaign.

Yet, jail time traumatized Adler. The madam had confidence that she could always beat the legal system now began to have doubts, fears and insecurities. It didn't help Polly's state of mind to learn that the police had tapped her phone when she moved into her new apartment on East 54th Street. The cops were still after her. The experience of being under constant scrutiny was getting old. Still Polly felt lucky. When the State of New York launched another corruption investigation in 1936 under Special Prosecutor Thomas Dewey, the police raided bordellos, rounding up and arresting call girls. Despite the crackdown, Polly was never arrested or called as a witness. But her friend, Lucky Luciano, was busted.

POLLY REMAINED IN the prostitution business until the early 1940s, opening and closing her bordello many times. Polly, however, had become disillusioned about the business, and her heart was not in it any more. In 1941 she was arrested for the

17th and final time, but the judge dismissed the charge because the prosecution failed to establish a case against her. In 1943, the Teflon Madam retired from the sex racket altogether and moved to Burbank, California, where she completed high school at age 50 and enrolled in college courses. In 1953, Polly Adler published her best selling autobiography, *A House is Not a Home*. In 1964, a forgettable film starring Shelley Winters as Polly brought the legendary madam's life to the big screen. In 1962, Polly Adler died of pancreatic cancer. When the Museum of Sex opened up in New York City in 1964, its premier exhibit included material on the legendary life and career of Pearl "Polly" Adler.

It was a remarkable life for a woman who once said of herself: "I'm one of those people who just can't help getting a kick even when it's a kick in the teeth."

The Queen of the Bootleggers

IN JANUARY 1920, while Polly Adler was still a teenager laboring in a sweat factory, Congress enacted a law that had a profound effect on the U.S. On December 10, 1913, Congress passed the Eighteenth Amendment, a measure that imposed a nationwide ban in the United States or its territories on the manufacture and transportation of intoxicating liquor with an alcohol content of at least .5 percent. After Nebraska became the required thirty-sixth state in the Union to ratify the Eighteenth Amendment, Congress sent the measure to President Woodrow Wilson for his signature. Wilson supported laws that encouraged moderation in alcohol consumption rather than a complete ban, and he vetoed the measure. Wilson's view, though, was in the minority, and Congress voted to override the measure. On January 17, 1920, Congress enacted the National Protection Enforcement Act, more commonly known as the Volstead Act, naming the law after Andrew Volstead, chairman of the House Judiciary Committee, which oversaw its passage.

The prohibitionists were ecstatic. The era of the "Noble Experiment" had begun. Evangelist Billy Sunday, one of America's highest-profile Prohibition advocates, held a mock funeral for alcoholic beverages at which he praised Prohibition.

Sunday predicted: "Saloons will soon be only a memory. We will turn our prisons into factories and our jails into storehouses and corncribs."

But if only Prohibition enforcement could have been so easy. In reality, the Volstead Act was confusing and ambiguous. Intoxicating liquors were defined as having more than .5 percent alcohol content, but alcohol with lower than the .5 percent level could still be sold. Liquor used for medicinal, sacramental, or industrial purposes was legal, no matter the alcohol content. Likewise fruit or grape beverages containing alcohol and prepared at home were legal.

Prohibition's economic consequences were not confusing, though, and that became another sure indicator that the "Noble Experiment" would be difficult to enforce. Overnight, 1,207 breweries, which served 178,000 saloons nationwide and created thousands of jobs, padlocked their doors.

The Volstead Act may have been the law of the land, but that did not deter millions of Americans from simply ignoring it. In his memoir, *Needle in the Haystack*, federal narcotics agent William J. Spillard recalled his visit to Miami in the early 1920s: "I took a sight-seeing bus out to see a new realty development. The bus driver asked me if I could use a bottle. A woman next to me on the bus wanted to sell me some liquor, and even the real estate salesman, after he had done his best to sell me a lot, turned around and asked: 'Well, can I interest you in some liquor?' That was the situation in Miami after fifty prohibition agents had been hard at work for three months."

THE BUSINESS OF smuggling alcoholic beverages to the U.S. to circumvent Prohibition and its laws became known as "rum-running." People from all walks of life wanted a piece of the Prohibition action, and they used every type of boat, from fishing vessel to private yacht, to smuggle the contraband into the United States. Louis A. Nula, a marine engineer and boat builder, designed a fast 30 to 40 foot boat, costing about $12,000 to $14,000 and powered by Liberty engines manufactured for World War I aircraft that were never made. After the war, Nula was able to buy the liberty engines for a song, which were used to equip speedy vessels called "rum boats."

MOST OF THE rum runners were men and included several colorful personalities who became as well known to the American public in the 1920s and early '30s as sports personalities are recognized today. Tea totaling Bill McCoy was immortalized in Ripley's popular syndicated newspaper column "Believe it or Not." James Horace Alderman was a Miami-based rum runner who died on the gallows in 1929 as a result of his rum-running activities. Duncan Red Shannon, Miami's favorite rumrunner, was shot dead by coast guardsman in a chase off the Florida coast.

One of the most famous rum runners, however, was a woman, a tall thin stately lady who was always impeccably dressed and who always carried a gun. It is said Gertrude Lythgoe was given the nickname "Cleo" because people thought her exotic looks made her a dead ringer for Queen Cleopatra. Later, she would be known as "The Queen of the Bahamas."

Netley Lucas, a young Englishman, vividly described the first time he saw Gertrude Lythgoe in the Bahamas: "I remember very distinctly our first sight of her on a hot tiring day. Among the rank and file swarthy-skinned, eager-eyed, and for the most part oddly-dressed individuals, she moved easily and gracefully, quietly observing the many faces which passed, generally speaking, just below the level of her eyes. Most striking of all about her in these surroundings and in such a setting was the extraordinary clearness of her skin and the intense darkness of her hair, which was extremely abundant and coiled closely and smoothly around her head. Her eyes were grey, beautifully shaped, and deeply set in a face as remarkable for its beauty as for its repose and quiet strength."

In the heart of Prohibition, Gertrude Lythgoe's exploits became legendary and the subject of much media scrutiny. The dailies, tabloids and magazines all ran stories about her, as the public seemed interested in her every move. Indeed, the media darlings of today would have been envious.

GERTRUDE "CLEO" LYTHGOE was born in Bowling Green, Ohio, the tenth child out of whom only six survived. Her father was a successful glass manufacturer, but one night the factory caught fire and burned to the ground. The family moved to St. Louis, but bad luck dogged the Lythgoe family. First, Gertrude's mother died. Then one of her sisters went totally deaf. Finally, her father decided he could not care for six children, and he placed the deaf child in a school for the deaf and Gertrude and the younger of her two brothers in orphanages.

Gertrude's aunt who lived in Greenfield, Indiana, was fond of Gertrude, and she got Gertrude's father's permission to allow the young girl to live with her. Gertrude was the first to agree that had not been the easiest child to care for.

"She (the aunt) did not realize what a problem child she would get," Gertrude later recalled. "Aunt had not known that even as a child, I developed wanderlust and was constantly wondering away and getting lost. The police finally suggested that my mother keep a tag around my neck showing my name and address."

One day the aunt received a letter from Gertrude's father informing her that he would be collecting his family and taking them with him to northern Indiana where he was building another glass factory. The father, however, was, by now, an alcoholic and lost his business. Margaret, the oldest child in the family, took charge and moved with Gertrude to Anderson, Indiana, where she enrolled Gertrude in parochial school.

Misfortune, however, continued to plague the Lythgoes. The father died. Despite his profligate ways, his death shocked Gertrude and she took it hard. She decided a change of scenery was in order and began traveling to Europe, Hawaii and the U.S. West Coast.

At her hotel in San Francisco, she met an English man who was in the timber business and wanted to return to England to start his own company. He asked Gertrude to move to England and work for him as a liaison secretary. Gertrude mulled the offer carefully since it would mean a big change in her life. But always the adventurer, she accepted the offer and moved to England.

At first, the work hours were unusually long and the office always seemed hectic, but, eventually, the timber business slowed down and the company began looking for other commodities to import and export. When business picked up again, the company opened up a New York office and Gertrude was headed for the Big Apple.

BY THIS TIME, Prohibition was in full swing and the demand for liquor boomed. Gertrude's company was approached about being an exporter of alcohol from England to the Bahamas. The company asked Gertrude to be its representative in the Bahamas, and she was on the move again, this time to Nassau, where she set up the company's wholesale liquor business on Market Street.

During Prohibition, much of the illegal booze poured into America from the Bahamas, a 600-mile archipelago of some 500 coral islands and keys, the closest located a mere 60 miles from the South Florida coast. With its numerous inlets, coves, rivers, and mango swamps, the Bahamas has a shoreline topography that makes it ideal for liquor smuggling. British, Canadian, European, and Jamaican distilleries sent huge shipments of rum, rye, gin, whiskey, cognac, scotch, and other assorted liquors to the Bahamas, where they were stored in huge warehouses on the docks until ready for transport to the U.S.

Nothing much happened in the Bahamas—that is, until the United States adopted Prohibition. In a 1926 *Saturday Evening Post* article, Walter Green, a Prohibition investigator for the U.S. government, described the principal industries of pre-Prohibition Bahamas as "pulling sponges off the roads and working for the American tourist who turned up each winter."

The Bahamas had a budget deficit before American Prohibition, Green pointed out in his article, but the economic situation had changed dramatically in the five years since he last visited. The country no longer had a debt and no longer was underdeveloped. Nassau, the Bahamian capital, now had electric lights, paved roads, hotels, golf courses, and curio shops. On the low hills behind the city one could see ostentatious castle-like homes belonging to prosperous liquor dealers with names like Christie, Kelly, and Collins, individuals who were making fortunes from Prohibition.

It is difficult to calculate the profits of the liquor dealers, but according to an official U.S. Coast Guard history, "enormous profits were to be made, with reports of 700 percent or more (profit) for the popular scotch or cognac." The public record revealed that American Prohibition had substantially boosted the Bahamian economy.

In 1918 the Bahamas received 20,654 gallons of liquor from Great Britain alone. Five years later, the number of imported gallons skyrocketed to 518,163 gallons, a twenty-five-fold increase. The Bahamian government collected a duty of $5.84 a case (a dozen quarts) from all the liquor smuggled into the United States. Before Prohibition, this figure amounted to about $90,000, but by 1926 that figure had jumped to $3.5 million, a forty-fold increase.

Walter Green pointed out that this figure was only the tax, not the total value of the liquor. "The Bahamian government is shaking down resident bootleggers to the tune of more than $3 million a year," Green reported. "Not bad pickings for a scattered fringe of coral reefs with a population of 58,000, more than 80 percent of whom are black."

In Bimini, the closest point in the Bahamas to mainland United States, one could see so-called Bimini boats dotting the port. About 25 feet in length, these boats could carry 400 cases of liquor and reach the shore of Florida in two hours. During Prohibition, the legal limits of U.S. territorial waters varied from 3 to 12 miles. So long as the ships stayed outside this line in international waters, the U.S. Coast Guard could not arrest their crews. The line of demarcation was called the "rum line," and the place where the ships collected, sometimes as many as a hundred at a time, "rum row." There were rum rows operating off the coast of Florid as well as New York and New Jersey.

Smaller, faster boats would go out beyond the rum line, load up the booze from the larger vessels, and then dash to Florida. The run could resemble a gauntlet. Hijackers lurked, looking for an opportunity to "pirate" the contraband at sea, while the Coast

Guard patrolled the Florida coast. And if the smugglers did make it to shore, thugs could be hiding in the shadows looking for an opportunity to steal their contraband.

Author Patricia Buchanan described the cat-and-mouse game that played out between the law and the rum runners: "For the most part, the men engaged in the liquor smuggling were experienced seamen who knew the tricky Florida-Bahamas waters and the myriad hiding places along the Miami shoreline. Lookouts, often local fishermen, told a rum-runner when the Coast Guard was nearby. He would stash his cargo in a mangrove swamp and suddenly become just another innocent fisherman."

If the smuggling trip was successful, some of the booze would be transported to the hotels, restaurants, and bootleggers of Miami and other points in southern Florida. Shipments were also smuggled north to other parts of the country in camouflaged barrels of fish or crates of citrus fruit and other produce.

THE CENTER OF the Nassau liquor business was the Lucerne Hotel, a three story frame structure that had about 50 rooms and was situated on Frederick Street. The media nicknamed the Lucerne "Bootlegger's Headquarters." One writer described the Lucerne as the site of "many a lively party and orgy."

The Bahamas liquor trade attracted an interesting and mostly mix of characters, adventurers, criminals and entrepreneurs and many of them stayed at the Lucerne Hotel.

Gertrude later wrote in her memoirs: "All types and nationalities converged on the front veranda (of the Lucerne) waiting or the ringing of the dinner bell. Many newspaper reporters and feature writers sat by the hour gathering rich material to be woven into fiction."

The Lucerne was owned by an American nurse named Dorothy Donnelle, who had previously worked in an insane asylum in Indiana. Gertrude called Donnelle "Mother" and remembered her as the "confidante" of most of her guests.

Guests included Tony, a scion of a wealthy family who spoke several languages and was rarely sober; a dignified but haughty representative of an English tobacco company; a man from Palm Beach, Florida, who was known socially as the "Count" and whom Gertrude remembered as a "parasite;" and a cowboy named Tex, who loved women and partying.

Gertrude Lythgoe fit in well with this motley group. She was young but had charisma and made a positive impression on people. One local reporter described her as "a truly wonderful personality, a woman of cultured tastes, who can talk on books and who travels with the best music in her trunks and shows such artistic taste in dress…"

Gertrude found the Bahamas assignment to be challenging. The company sent another representative and a young assistant to help, but they were lazy and had no initiative. Gertrude had to look hard to find reliable help, but she concluded that she was better off working by herself. Compounding the challenge—she did not own a lorry and so was forced to hire less efficient local donkey carts.

One time the lack of able assistance cost her dearly. Without Gertrude's knowledge and approval and in her absence, a friend of hers, whom she identified simply as "Duke," had sent a cable to her company's London office requesting them to send a thousand cases of whiskey. Duke thought he had worked out a great deal, but the buyers did not put up any security for the merchandise. It was a red flag Duke should have seen. When

Duke informed Gertrude of the deal, she immediately suspected it was scam, but could do little about it. The crooks absconded with the liquor.

Gertrude was in a business where, as she put it: "The buyers were not a class mentioned in the social register."

It was tough being a lady in such company. Often, she would leave a meeting when the language got rough and crude, but her many competitors stayed on, and this gave them an advantage. Some people found it hard to believe a young American girl would be off on her own, representing a British firm, and rumors flew about how she could be a secret agent for the U.S.

In an interview with writer H. De Winton Wigley for his book *With the Whiskey Smugglers*, Gertrude confided: "I got to hear of this talk and I took steps to show that they were quite wrong. I know I was discussed a great deal but they finally accepted me."

NO QUESTION IT was tough for Gertrude to operate in the macho world of the Bahamas liquor business. At one point, it looked as if her competitors were conspiring to prevent her from selling her goods. One time, she had to make the annual renewal of her liquor license, which she needed to operate in the Bahamas. One official, who was friends with one of Gertrude's biggest competitors, objected to the license renewal. The competitor's lackey accused Gertrude of keeping company with a man who had threatened his life. It was a ridiculous charge, but Gertrude had to defend herself if she wanted her license renewed. Usually, buyers had a lawyer to take care of the renewal, but Gertrude handled her own application.

She spoke for fifteen minutes in her defense, telling the Liquor Control Board: "Suppose I make a like charge against this very official because he refused to marry some woman. What has this to do with any liquor license? Nothing, the board agreed, and Gertrude's license was renewed.

Gertrude was not afraid to take matters in her own hands. She told De Winton Wigley how she handled one man who said derogatory things about her whiskey:

"Every one knows my liquor is the very best. But for some reason or another, this man thought he would criticize it to other people, and he always said something unpleasant about me. Well I found him in a barbershop with his face lathered, and I just walked right in and told I wanted to talk to him. I fetched him along to my office, and there I just warned him. I told him I'd put a bullet through him as sure as he sat there. He went away mighty quick."

Frustrated by the stone wall, Gertrude told Duke, her friend: "Here we are with the very stock the market is greedy for and buyers a plenty waiting for goods we have—of which there is little to be had—and still we make no sale. It seems to me this is a case of boycotting. We have to devise some means of escape or the London office is in for a big loss."

GERTRUDE'S SITUATION BEGAN changing when she heard about the arrival in the Nassau port of a ship under the command of Bill McCoy, a former Florida boat builder and one of rum running's biggest personalities. McCoy began his criminal career hauling rum from Bimini to Miami and made a fortune in rum running. He established the smuggling system whereby ships would anchor off the U.S. coast in international waters and sell the liquor to smaller ships, which would then transfer the cargo to the shore. McCoy's fair dealing and commitment to selling quality liquor are said to have spawned the phrase "The Real McCoy." In the 1940s Robert Ripley immortalized McCoy in his hugely popular syndicated newspaper column, "Believe It or Not." Gertrude had never met McCoy but had heard of him and his legendary exploits in the rum running trade and knew of his reputation for being a good and honest business man.

After a few successful trips smuggling liquor, McCoy had made enough made money to buy the schooner Arethusa at auction, placing it under British registry to avoid being subject to U.S. law. McCoy later changed the name of his schooner to Tomoka.

Gertrude instructed Duke to find McCoy, give him a sample of her liquor and tell him she would guarantee it to be as good as any liquor he had in his cargo. The Duke did not have to work hard to do that. Gertrude's reputation for the quality of the goods she sold had preceded her emissary. McCoy told Duke that he knew all about the good quality of Gertrude's goods. Her competitors are scared to death, McCoy revealed, so she must be selling superior liquor or else they would not be hell bent on driving her out of business.

"I'll drop by Miss Lythgoe's office in the morning," McCoy informed Duke.

The next morning, Gertrude finally met with the Real McCoy. She was quite impressed: The blue-eyed rum running legend was tall, well built, and immaculately dressed in white doeskin trousers and a white shirt. He held a white helmet in his hand. When Gertrude offered McCoy a cigarette, he told her he neither smoked nor drank.

"He was outstanding, the very opposite of the types I had been meeting," Gertrude later recalled. The Queen of the Bootleggers was smitten. "Something hit me hard. I could not materialize just what it was."

For maybe the only time in her life, Gertrude felt intimidated by a man, and she wondered if she could deal with him.

McCoy told her that a merchant with whom he was working didn't have his goods ready for export. If Gertrude left her goods on consignment with him, he could sell them for her. Gertrude could even accompany her cargo, if she wanted. Gertrude asked Duke, who attended the meeting, what he thought.

"It's a great idea," the Duke said.

But Gertrude did not have enough cash on hand to pay the duty and get her shipment of rye whiskey released. No problem, McCoy assured her. He had enough cash on hand to cover the duty. He would deduct the expense from the money Gertrude received for her goods. Gertrude agreed to the deal.

"We will leave the next day at noon," McCoy instructed. "Don't tell anybody you are coming along."

Gertrude gave McCoy a check to pay the duty. Gertrude's deal with McCoy came at the most opportune time, for her back was against the wall and she did not really have a choice. Her competitors had almost succeeded in putting her out of business. She was not going to let that happen, though, nor was she going to let her company down.

IT WAS A hot July 4th day when the Tomoka set out for sea with a cargo of 5, 510 cases of rye, gin, bourbon and some beer and champagne. For the woman liquor supplier, the trip was full of uncertainty, and she wondered what fate awaited her and her cargo. She knew nothing about sailing a ship, and as crew members scurried about the ship, busy with their duties, she felt useless. She was the only woman on board and she wondered where she would sleep. The ship had only one cabin.

"Try as I did, I could not pity myself and could not keep back the tears, which relieved my nervous tension and pent up feelings," Gertrude recalled in her memoir. "The last I remembered that night was myself silent(ly) weeping."

Yet, during the journey, McCoy became as impressed with Gertrude as she was with him. In Frederick Van de Water's book, The Real McCoy, McCoy remembered Gertrude as "a thoroughly competent woman of whom no man could make passes with impunity. She expected others to mind their own business as she attended to hers."

IT TOOK SIX days for the McCoy's ship to reach rum row, where it waited for the speed boats to arrive so deals could be made. Finally, the speed boats came. Some of them bought a few cases of liquor, while others bought them by the hundreds. The buyers used assumed names or nicknames. Nobody asked questions. Once the deal was consummated the buyers were quickly gone.

After Gertrude sold her cargo, a buyer, whom she had seen a number of times in Nassau, offered to take her ashore in his boat free of charge. Normally, the trip would cost $100, so Gertrude accepted the kind offer. After three weeks at sea, she was once again back on shore, exhausted but happy. She received her money and went to the bank to make a big deposit. Her trip had been a big gamble, but it paid off.

Her company's home office in London had not heard from her in three weeks, but they were delighted to learn that Gertrude had sold the big load. She was instructed to return to London to give a full report. At a meeting, the company's board of directors gave her a vote of thanks, 500 shares of stock in the company and a percentage of the profits. The company now knew that Gertrude could do the job and it instructed her that, after returning to Nassau, she should go to Cuba where another shipment of goods was sitting in transit waiting for delivery.

Many of the Nassau folk admired Gertrude for the gamble she took, and she returned to the Bahamas a celebrity. Her fame spread far beyond the Bahamas. One article appeared in *London Daily News* newspaper along with a photograph of her and a headline in big black letters underneath that read: "With the whiskey smugglers; Cleopatra, Queen of the Bootleggers."

She received thousands of letters from all types of people in many different walks of life—businessmen, British royalty, housewives and even prisoners. Some asked for autographs. Others criticized her for being in the liquor business. A few proposed marriage. Others asked her to make an investment in their business schemes.

Eventually, though, the fame got old. "The limelight became a nuisance to me," Gertrude later recalled. "The tourist season was in full swing and everybody knew me. They glared, stared, tried to take snap shots and became so bothersome that my nerves almost snapped under the strain."

GERTRUDE DECIDED THAT she had no reason to stay in Nassau any longer. When it was time to go, she left like a member of royalty. The locals held plenty of lunches and dinners in her honor, and her friends went to the dock to see her off. On the day of departure, an English major who was engaged in some kind of government dredging work, dipped the colors in salute.

Gertrude recalled: "As we sailed by the dredge and I waved goodbye, he has prearranged the salute as a surprise to me."

Gertrude arrived in Coconut Grove, Miami, where she stayed with friends. In a bizarre incident, a police officer arrested her in a department store for allegedly cashing two bad checks: One for $6 and the other for $8. It was a case of mistaken identity, and when Gertrude and her lawyer appeared before the court, Gertrude was identified as Gertrude Lythgoe and the case was dismissed.

Gertrude's troubles, however, were not over. She was served with a warrant, charging her with conspiracy to smuggle one thousand cases of whisky into New Orleans. The Queen of the Bootleggers had to post a $1,000 bond before being extradited from Miami to New Orleans for federal trial. A U.S. Assistant Attorney in New Orleans released Gertrude on her own recognizance and told her she that she would have to appear for trial in several weeks. When the trial came, Gertrude not only acted as her own defense lawyer, she took the witness stand and was cross examined. For Gertrude the trial was a bitter pill to swallow. Her friend, Duke, turned state's evidence and testified against her. But the charges against her were thrown out of court and she was released.

IN 1945, GERTRUDE met Bill McCoy one last time. She was in Boston when she received a telegram from McCoy urging her to come to nearby Gloucester and see him. The Federal authorities had caught McCoy and he had spent nine years in prison for rum running. Now he was living a quiet, straight and narrow life.

Gertrude took the train and found McCoy on his old schooner. They embraced, talked about old times and spent a few hours touring the schooner and McCoy's yacht, named the Whiz. McCoy tried to convince Gertrude to stay for a few weeks, but she declined, telling her old friend that she had to attend to unfinished business.

Before Gertrude left, McCoy got her to promise to go with him on a long trip to the South Seas. The unexpected visit looked as if it would lead to romance, but it would be the last time Gertrude saw McCoy. He died of a heart attack on December 30, 1948.

Gertrude returned to Miami and established permanent residence at Parkleigh House. She eventually resided in New York City, and for 25 years lived at the Tiller Hotel in Grand Circus Park in Detroit, Michigan. Gertrude found success in the legitimate business world, owning a successful rent-a-car business, and it was said that she held the patent to the mileage theft insurance lock that were installed on rental cars. She also reportedly owned property in Detroit and Evansville, Indiana. *The Wall Street Journal* estimated Gertrude's fortune to be in the millions, but no one know for sure how much money she was worth at her death.

On June 24, 1974, Gertrude Lythgoe died in Los Angeles, California, at age 86. Gertrude is believed to be the inspiration for the 1975 movie "Lucky Lady," starring Liza Minelli, Burt Reynolds and Gene Hackman. In the comedy, Hackman, Minnelli and Reynolds are Depression-era bootleggers who form an awkward love triangle. Escaping both the law and a murderous gang of rival crooks, the threesome set sail on a small boat called the "Lucky Lady."

Gertrude Lythgoe never married, but it is believed she carried a torch for Bill McCoy until the day she died.

THREE

The Numbers Queen

I N 1912 A remarkable woman named Stephanie St. Clair arrived in Harlem, New York from Marseilles, France. The details of St. Clair's life are sketchy, but it is believed she was born in Martinique, a small island in the Caribbean region, and was about 26 years old when she landed. The young woman arrived in Harlem at a time of great change. Prior to 1910, few African Americans lived within the present day borders of Harlem, for the neighborhood was a destination point for a diverse group of European ethnic groups, including the Dutch, Germans, Italians, Jews and Irish. Real estate speculation in Harlem had led to a major development boon, but the expected migration of white tenants did not materialize, and many of the newly constructed buildings remained unoccupied.

Philip Payton, Jr., an enterprising Black Harlem realtor, saw how he could turn an economic bust into a money making venture, and he convinced whites tenants to rent their long vacant apartments to blacks. Still, the migration of blacks to Harlem was a trickle. In an era of hard core segregation, whites resisted this migration, but then gave up the fight, sold their property and left Harlem.

By the time St. Clair arrived, Harlem was emerging as a black metropolis. Ironically, a few years later, when the advent of Prohibition brought a national ban on the sale of alcohol, Harlem became a prime destination for the Mafia's bootleg booze, and Harlem boomed as prime entertainment hot spot crammed with trendy nightclubs and cabarets, must see venues for whites from other neighborhoods in the Big Apple and visitors from around the world.

Harlem had something for every kind of taste and social class. Throngs of white people trekked to the neighborhood by taxi, private car, limousine and subway, hopping from one hot venue to another. Nightclubs like Connie's Inn, Paradise and the Cotton Club made Harlem world famous, as white voyeurs were able to observe exotic entertainment and imbibe booze without, to any appreciable degree, crossing the segregated color line.

IN THIS JIM Cow environment, St. Clair found opportunity. It is not clear how St. Clair did it, but it is believed she had accumulated $10,000 by 1922. In their book, *Harlem Godfather*, authors Mayme Johnson and Karen Quinones Miller noted that: "St. Clair never spoke about how she raised the capital, but her detractors reminded people that her title was after all Madam."

What is certain is that St. Clair used the money to launch a number operation that would make her a legend in Harlem. The numbers racket has long history in the black and Hispanic neighborhoods of the Big Apple, as well as other major American cities. Traditionally the numbers game has been based on lottery policy numbers (12 numbers drawn from a pool of 78), which was determined by a complex drawing requiring a structured organization to figure out the winning numbers.

But during the early 1920s, at the time St. Clair was getting into the racket, the rules of the game had changed considerably.

The betting scheme was simplified, and the winning numbers selected became based on the daily closing results of the New York Stock Exchange. The winning total paid at 600 to one, and the beauty of the new system was that by having the numbers recorded daily in the newspaper, the game could not be fixed.

For a mere 10-cent bet, a numbers player could make $60, a sizeable return in the Harlem of the 1920s, which was one of the poorest neighborhoods in New York City. The numbers racket became a strong tradition in the neighborhood, and even though it was a nickel-and-dime game, people from all economic backgrounds played. One observer described the game as "the most widespread form of law breaking in Harlem…"

Entering the numbers racket at the right time, the charismatic St. Clair thrived in that underworld environment and did quite well for herself. By the late 1920s, she was using 20 controllers and 40 numbers runners to haul in an estimated $350,000 annually, making her one of the richest—if not the richest—black woman in America.

Queenie's personality was as full as her pocketbook, and it was with good reason that Stephanie St. Clair became known as "Queenie." She could be flamboyant, brazen, or generous, and as unpredictable as stormy weather. At 5'8", she was a husky but attractive woman. Old-timers from Harlem would later remember St. Clair as having an imperious presence and as being an aficionado of the finer things of life, which included cloths and the Opera. Given her fiery and fearless nature, Harlemites would also refer to St. Clair as the "Tiger from Marseilles." No doubt, she was the type of person, man or woman, you wanted on your side when the going got tough.

She lived like a queen should, at the famous 409 Edgecombe, with the cream of Harlem society. The E-shaped, 13-story red brick apartment building was situated high up on Sugar Hill, above the Harlem River and Hudson Valley overlooking the Bronx and Lower Manhattan. In the 1930s and '40s, 409 Edge-combe was the home of such prominent African-Americans as W.E.B. Du Bois, Walter White and Thurgood Marshall.

Thelma Wilson, who managed the building, beginning in 1927, remembered St. Clair "breezing through the lobby with her fur coat dramatically flowing behind her," and wearing "exotic dresses with a colorful turban wrapped around her head."

Like many in Harlem, Wilson was impressed with Queenie's "courage, intelligence, skill and savvy."

This, however, is not how Hollywood has portrayed this larger-than-life personality. Queenie appears as a character in the 1997 movie, "Hoodlum," which stars Laurence Fishburne, Andy Garcia and Cicely Tyson as St. Clair and provides a fictional account of white organized crime's attempt to take over the Harlem's numbers racket in the early 1930s. In the movie, St. Clair is portrayed as weak and submissive to Bumpy Johnson, the movie's main black character, the hero who must take on the white Mob. St. Clair effectively disappears early in the movie.

In real life, Queenie was no shrinking violet. In 1935, the Policy Queen entered into an "odd couple" marriage with Sufi Abdul Hamid, a colorful and dynamic guru of sorts who had arrived in Harlem from Chicago in 1930. The charismatic Hamid was an imposing presence on the streets of Harlem. He had close-cropped hair, a brown beard and piercing eyes, and dressed in flowing robes, turban, cape and riding boots.

Hamid claimed to be of Egyptian ancestry, but he claimed to be a lot of things.

Biographers believe his real name was Eugene Brown, and he was probably born in Philadelphia, Pennsylvania. While later living in the Windy City, Hamid made fiery speeches and led several boycotts of white owned businesses in Chicago's black neighborhoods that refused to hire blacks. With Harlem experiencing higher than 50 percent unemployment rates during the Great Depression, Hamid's road show did not miss a beat. His message that blacks needed to organize economically struck a chord with the locals and he recruited a significant number of followers. But when Hamid appealed to blacks to "drive the Jews out of Harlem," he was vilified and accused of being a "Black Hitler," and his message was drowned in controversy.

Actually, Queenie and Hamid had more in common than just the turbans they wore. She, too, was a militant black nationalist who urged Haitian Americans to stick up for their rights. She opened the French Legal Aid Society, and "urged her fellow immigrants to qualify and become registered voters to stamp out corruption."

Not much is known about the marriage, except that it was brief and almost ended in sudden death. Queenie suspected Hamid of having an affair with a buxom spiritualist named Madame Fulton. In a rage, Queenie pulled out a gun and fired at her cheating spouse; fortunately, she missed. Hamid went on to marry Fulton, while Queenie's temper got her five to ten years in prison. In August, 1938, Hamid was killed in a plane crash. *The New York Times* headline read: "Plane Crash Fatal to Harlem's Hitler."

IN GROWING HER numbers business, Queenie was soon knee deep in corruption New York style. When a police officer from the NYPD's Sixth Division threatened to arrest her, Queenie scoffed and told him that he had nothing to support the charge. The policeman suggested that they go to the 123rd

Street Station and talk it over with his superior, the lieutenant. She agreed and met the lieutenant, who explained the nitty-gritty of how the streets of Harlem worked.

St. Clair fell in line, greasing the lieutenant's palm with a $300 payoff delivered via a courier named "Mustache Jones." From that day on, Queenie began to send regular payments of $100 and $500 to an anonymous cop, whom she believed to be the corrupt lieutenant. The mysterious recipient was nice enough to call the Policy Queen after each payment to inform her he had received it, thank you. In all, she paid the police officers attached to the West 123rd Street Station a total of $6,000.

The police, however, did not leave her alone. They kept harassing and arresting her runners, even as she made the payments like clockwork. The police, moreover, were demanding more and more money. Queenie was a proud woman, and she took it personally. The last straw was when she suspected that a cop had broken into her home and stolen $500. The intruder had cut his hand and left some bloody fingerprints on the windowsill. Queenie telephoned the corrupt lieutenant and demanded that the police arrest and punish the intruder.

"It would be an easy case to solve," she urged. "After all, he left a fingerprint behind."

Nothing happened. St. Clair pestered the police, but they ignored her. The Numbers Queen was outraged and fed up. If the rats would not cooperate, she would sink the ship and expose them to the public. Queenie shook up Harlem when she placed several paid advertisements in the *Amsterdam News*, the neighborhood's major newspaper, accusing the police of corruption. She even wrote letters to Mayor Jimmy Walker and President Franklin D. Roosevelt.

In one letter to Mayor Walker, she wrote: "Sometimes, detectives find policy slips in their search, but if you pay them from $500 to $2,000, you are sure to come back home. If you pay them nothing, you are sure to get a sentence from 60 to 90 days in the work house."

In a community battered and bruised by the corrupt white establishment, Queenie became a folk hero.

On December 31, 1930, at 11:00 a.m., St. Clair left home and caught a bus. Immediately she felt as if someone were following her. When she got off and entered 177 West 141st Street, three policemen rushed her and arrested her after allegedly finding policy slips in her possession.

"I was framed," St. Clair told anyone who would listen. She vowed: "I will fight them legally to the finish... and I will never stop."

St. Clair was convicted on a gambling charge and spent eight months of a two-year sentence in the workhouse on Welfare Island.

IN 1931, THE Seabury Commission began an investigation into the massive corruption in New York City's government. Named after Judge Samuel Seabury, a crusading crime investigator and scion of a prominent New York City family, the investigation lasted two years and probed the relationship between police, politicians and gangsters. Stephanie St. Clair was one of the star witnesses, testifying that she ran a numbers bank from 1923 to 1928 and ended up paying bribes totaling about $7,100 to members of the police department. It was done, she said, to protect her workers from arrest. Queenie did not hold back her punches.

In her autobiography, *Strangers at the Party*, Helen Lawrenson explained: "St. Clair accused a district attorney, two judges, and scores of police, bondsmen, and political fixers. She gave names, dates, and the amount paid out in graft."

Her testimony helped get a police lieutenant and 30 other police officers suspended from duty. The brash St. Claire gave a warning to Tammany Hall: "Many more… will be in the same predicament if they do not stop framing colored people."

Although St. Claire's high-profile public utterances drew the attention of the white power structure, it appears that the Harlem community largely supported her. After her Seabury Commission testimony, Queenie felt vindicated, but still had to go into hiding, fearing retaliation.

Corruption in Tammany Hall was not the only topic of inquiry for the Seabury Commission. A number of major Harlem numbers bankers were compelled to testify, and under close scrutiny, their revelations cast further light on the lucrative Harlem numbers racket. Several numbers kings had to reveal their incomes from the racket, and the figures were eye-opening. For instance, by examining the personal bank accounts of one numbers runner, Jose Enrique Miro, the Seabury Commission learned that, in six of his nine accounts, Miro had deposited $1,111,730; in the other three, another $139,826. He became big enough to be called one of the six major policy bankers in Harlem.

Wilfred Adolphus Brunder, had a bad reputation for not paying players when their numbers came in, but he still was making $3,000 to $4,000 daily. Brunder deposited in various accounts $1,753,342.33 of unreported income between January 1, 1925 and December 31, 1931, according to the Seabury Commission investigation. To avoid prosecution for tax evasion, both

Miro and Bruner, as well another numbers king named Panama Francis, fled the U.S. Francis did so to his native Granada with a reported $1 million.

The public could see that the Harlem numbers game was mushrooming in profitability, even as the Great Depression destroyed the local economy. People were eager to use their nickels and dimes to buy a policy and get the one big hit that would change their lives. Given the money involved, it would just be a matter of time, though, before a powerful white gangster would get smart and move into Harlem to organize the rackets. Any gangster with a little gray matter could discern that Prohibition would soon be over, and they would have to look for new rackets to corner. But who would that gangster be? The organizing force would be a ruthless gangster with a hair-trigger temper and a one-dollar haircut. Dutch Schultz, the same gangster who took over Polly Adler's apartment and made the New York City Madam's life hell, would make the numbers racket more profitable than it had ever been. Along the way, he would not have his way as he did with Polly Adler. Rather, he would have to deal with another charismatic queenpin named Stephanie St. Clair, who challenged his best-laid plans.

JUST LOOKING AT Schultz's reputation, one would conclude that he did not have the right stuff to be a big-time Mobster. He was not much to look at. Women who knew Dutch often described him as looking like "Bing Crosby with his nose bashed in."

He played by few rules himself, and his loose-cannon style of criminal management did not sit well with his Mafia colleagues. Schultz was a psychopath, and if he wanted something, he would simply take it at the point of a gun. He killed, if necessary, in the blink of an eye.

"Dutch was so ruthlessly unpredictable that most other bosses on the National Commission had to admit him to their ruling council," wrote Marvin J. Wolf and Katherine Mader. "It was the only way of exerting control over him. "

Schultz would usually get his way when he had to deal with other gangsters. Jack "Legs" Diamond was a New York City gangster who rose to prominence in the bootleg business. Schultz attempted to kill Legs several times and lost several men trying. Legs always seem to survive. One time, Legs took five bullets but lived, although he had to spend a few weeks in a hospital. In another murder attempt Legs took three bullet but survived again while two people passing by were killed. Schultz was heard to ask: "Ain't there nobody (sic) who can shoot this guy so that he don't bounce back?"

Finally, two gun men caught up with Legs while he lay passed out in a hotel room. The gun men picked Legs up, stood him against the wall and pumped two bullets into his head. The killers were never found, but it was a good bet that Schultz masterminded the hit.

While Mobsters feared Schultz, they also despised and dismissed him, considering him to be an embarrassment to their profession. For one thing, he was a tight wad. How tight? For starters, he made millions of dollars but bought his suits off the rack. *The New York Times* describes him as looking like an "ill dressed vagrant."

Mafia godfather Lucky Luciano once said of Schultz: "The guy has got a couple of million dollars and he dresses like a pig." The Dutchman paid his henchmen poorly, but would go into a rage when they complained or asked him for a raise.

Schultz's violent and brutal demeanor was deceptive. He was bright and organized and had a good mind for business. The Dutchman knew how to take advantage of business opportunities when he saw them.

SCHULTZ WAS BORN Arthur Flegenheimer on August 6, 1902, the son of German-Jewish immigrants. His father, Herman Flegenheimer, was a saloon keeper and livery stable owner. Arthur's mother Emma tried her best to get her son to grow up as a respectable citizen with a good job, but to no avail. When Schultz was 14, his father deserted the family, and the Dutchman quit school in the sixth grade to take odd jobs to help support the home. Even with his limited education, Schultz became an avid reader who devoured books and newspapers.

He once told a reporter why he took the name of Dutch Schultz: "It was short enough to fit the headlines. If I kept the name of Flegenheimer, nobody would have heard of me."

Hotheaded Schultz would go ballistic, though, over what was written about him in the newspapers. Myer Berger, *The New York Times* ace reporter, once described Dutch Shultz as a "pushover for blondes."

"What kind of language is that for *the New York Times*?" the gangster scolded Berger.

Three years after leaving school, Schultz was arrested for a burglary in the Bronx and was sent to reform school. He escaped but was caught 15 hours later and returned to prison to serve a 15-month term. That was the only occasion in Schultz's brief life that he served time, even though he eventually had 13 arrests for murder, assault and numerous other crimes.

In the early years of Prohibition, the Dutchman worked his way through the Bronx beer trade, organizing a gang that was based at East 149th Street and dominated the bootlegging and speakeasies in Harlem. Schultz and Joe Noe, his partner and friend, opened up the Hub Social Club in the Bronx. From there the Dutchman assembled a formidable crew of gunmen whom he used to intimidated businessmen and take over their businesses.

Eventually, Dutch became known as "the Beer Baron of the Bronx," but he was shrewd enough to realize that political connections were the key to staying on top in the criminal world. He formed an alliance with Jimmy Hines, a Democrat insider who was one of the most corrupt politicians in New York City history. Hines received $500 to $600 weekly from Schultz to protect the gangster's Harlem numbers racket and his bootleg operations.

IN THE WAKE of the Seabury investigations, Schultz made his move to conquer the Harlem numbers racket, employing the same strategy and ruthless efficiency that he used to muscle into the other rackets he dominated. As individual operators without firepower or real political connections, the black numbers kings were powerless to stop the white interloper. Schultz began picking off the big numbers bankers one by one. The first target was Big Joe Ison, who by this time was operating the banks of fugitives Miro and Brunder. One day, Abe Landau and Abe "Bo" Weinberg, two of Schultz's lieutenants, took Ison for a ride, put a gun to his ribs and told him he had to pay their boss protection money if he wanted to stay in business.

Not the coolest of gangsters, Ison was known as "Spasm" for the uncontrollable tic he got in the face when he got a good hand during a poker game. Spasm went to seek the advice of his attorney, 26-year-old J. Richard "Dixie" Davis, who specialized in handling policy cases. Despite his youth, Davis was known for being able to fix any problem in the racket. Unfortunately for Ison, Davis was close to Shultz and on his payroll.

He advised Ison to get in touch with Bo's brother George Weinberg, a former policy banker, to see what could be arranged. At the meeting with Weinberg, Ison realized he had been dealt a bad hand and agreed to pay Schultz $600 a week.

Now that he was being "protected," Ison came to Schultz with a problem. Miro was back in town and wanted his business. "Let me take care of it," Schultz told Ison and he arranged a late-night meeting with Miro. Miro was so agitated at the thought of a meeting with the godfather that he showed up clad only in silk pajamas and his overcoat. Miro readily agreed; he needed protection.

The big numbers bankers continued to move in lockstep. Patrick Downey explains the procedure: "The typical meeting consisted of the banker sitting in a room with a couple of Schultz's torpedoes. Then the Dutchman would enter flanked by two bodyguards. Schultz would take out his .45, place it on the table, and inform the banker he was now an employee of the Schultz organization."

THE DUTCHMAN MOVED forward in Harlem as if his main ambition was to turn the neighborhood into a plantation for organized crime. It did not matter to the gangster that it was the depths of the Great Depression and more than half of the locals were unemployed. People needed jobs desperately and they needed to keep them, but tough luck. Schultz began downsizing the rackets, eliminating the hardworking grunts—the numbers runners—from the game. He undercut them by opening up stores as fronts for betting where the bettors could buy their policy slips without having to pay a part of their winnings to the runner as they usually did. The Dutchman naïvely thought the community would support his plan, but Harlem was outraged. Not only was the community going to lose jobs, white gangsters were taking all the money out of the community. Harlem boycotted the white-owned stores until Schultz agreed to use the runners. It was one small victory for Harlem.

STEPHANIE ST. CLAIR refused to kowtow to the Dutchman, and she tried to convince the big bankers still outside the Dutchman's noose to band together and fight.

"No way," they said. How could they fight the Mob and City Hall at the same time? They were in cahoots.

So Queenie organized the smaller bankers who operated outside of Schultz's influence. She went to the Harlem newspapers and placed paid advertisements, announcing that outsiders were once again ripping off the community. She journeyed to the big metropolitan dailies and told her story. The rags liked her spunk but did little for her cause.

Queenie took her fight right to City Hall. Dutch Schultz biographer Paul Sann describes what happened when interim mayor Joseph V. McKee told his police aide Lieutenant James Harten to see the visitor from Harlem: "Madame Queen submitted that the Dutchman planned to put her on the spot and what did the city of New York propose to do about it? Lieutenant Harten said he would alert the police in Harlem to see that no harm befell her at the hands of Mr. Schultz or any ne'er-do-well."

Seeing the fat cat bureaucrats was a waste of time, so Queenie went back to Harlem and used some intimidation tactics of her own on the neighborhood's white shopkeepers, warning them not to collaborate with the Schultz organization.

"She entered their stores, one after another, and single-handedly smashed plate glass cases, snatched and destroyed policy slips, and ordered the 'small tiers' to get out of Harlem," wrote Irma Watkins Owens.

Queenie even informed authorities that the small tiers were selling policy slips to minors and helped to gather evidence to prove it.

THE DUTCHMEN WAS getting impatient with the troublemaker and put out a contract out on her life. Queenie went into hiding.

"I'm not afraid of Dutch Schultz or any man living," the Policy Queen declared. "He'll never touch me."

Schultz's men went looking for Queenie; the intense manhunt at one point forced her to hide in a coal cellar, where she lay buried under a pile of coal.

In her memoir of 409 Edgecombe, Katherine Butler Jones recounts a revealing anecdote about Queenie's battle with the Dutchman, told to her by Harold Thomas, who lived in apartment 13E. One day in the summer of 1931, Thomas saw a black limo pull up to 409 and four men get out.

"They were very businesslike in their appearance," Thomas recalled. "They about-faced and walked into the building military style. I took them up on the south elevator to Madame Stephanie's floor. They rang for me about twenty minutes later and repeated the routine, by leaving the same way as when they entered, without a saying a word."

"These men were Madame St. Clair's protectors. My cousin Billy Gardner, who lives on the first floor with his mother, told me that Dutch Schultz sent one of his men to see Madame St. Clair. She pushed him into the closet, locked the door and called her men to take care of him."

Queenie, it appeared, had protection as well, which may help explain why she was able to avoid the Dutchman's murderous clutches.

IN THE END, it was a losing battle for Harlem's kings and queens of the numbers racket. Schultz's fire power and Mob muscle were too much for Madam St. Clair and Harlem's would-be gangsters, and he was able to get the numbers securely under his control. St. Clair went to jail for shooting Hamid, effectively ending her involvement in the numbers racket.

Schultz had successfully organized the numbers racket, but he had a big problem. He was being hounded on tax evasion charges by a relentless young prosecutor named Thomas Dewey who, in the spring of 1935, put him on trial. The government had a good amount of evidence, but Schultz had great lawyers; the trial ended in a hung jury. Undaunted, Dewey retried Schultz, this time in the small northern New York town of Malone. The Dutchman moved to Malone and embarked on an aggressive public relations campaign to win the hearts and minds of the good citizens—and potential jurors—of the town.

The prosecution had a solid case once again, but in American jurisprudence evidence isn't everything. The normally cheap Dutchman spent money as if he had his own private mint, even buying beers in the local bar to show the town that he was regular Joe. The campaign worked: he was acquitted.

"It would be apparent to all who had followed the evidence on the case that you have reached the verdict based not on the evidence but on some other reason," the perturbed judge told the jury.

YET DUTCH SCHULTZ left Malone with his empire crumbling. The Harlem numbers racket had served as its cornerstone, but now Schultz heard that Dewey planned to go after it. The Dutchman knew what had to be done: he would kill the special prosecutor. That was the only way to get the man off his back. But it was not an easy thing to do. In the past four years, the Mob had put a national council in place, which decided such weighty matters, and the Dutchman would have to make a proposal to the most powerful Mobsters in America, including Lucky Luciano, Meyer Lansky, Vito Genovese, and Albert Anastasia. The council rejected Schultz's plan, not wanting to face the wrath of the Federal Government. Angry and frustrated, the Dutchman stormed out of the meeting, but left the distinct impression he would still carry out the hit himself. The council made a decision. The Dutchman was out of control and had to go.

On December 3, 1935, two hit men, Charlie "the Bug" Workman and Mendy Weiss, walked into the back of the Palace, a Newark, New Jersey bar and restaurant, where Dutch Schultz, with two of his body guards, was meeting with Otto "Abadabba" Berman. Workman and Weiss opened fire, killing Berman and one of the bodyguards, while leaving the other one dying. Noticing that Schultz was not with the other three, Workman went into the men's room, where he saw movement at the urinal and opened fire. It was the Dutchman. While Workman fled, Schultz staggered out of the john, headed for the table, and slumped into a chair. An ambulance rushed him to the Newark hospital.

The gangster was delirious and his incoherent verbal ramblings have become the stuff of Mob legend: "Please make it quick, fast and furious. Please, fast and furious." And "Oh, oh, dog biscuit. And when he is happy, he doesn't get snappy."

Dutch Schultz fell into a coma and died a few days later.

But before he died, the Dutchman received a telegram from Stephanie St. Clair. It read: "Don't be yellow. As you sow, shall you reap." Queenie had the last word in Harlem's battle royale.

Stephanie St. Clair eventually faded from history and little is known about the rest of her life. When Queenie died in 1969, the world did not take notice.

FOUR

Public Enemies

I N THE 1920S and early 1930s, organized crime dominated criminal activity, as the Mafia used Prohibition and its misguided laws to make a fortune in the bootlegging business. The rising merchants of crime included gangsters Lucky Luciano and Dutch Schultz who frequented Polly Adler's New York City bordello. Gertrude "Cleo" Lythgoe, the so called "Queen of the Bootleggers," made a lot of money serving the bootleggers who bought and peddled the booze that satisfied a thirsty American public. Meanwhile, after the Seabury Commission hearings in New York City in 1930, the Mafia began greedily eying the huge profits that black gangsters in Harlem were reaping from the numbers racket.

The 1929 Depression, however, gave rise to a new class of criminal with names like John Dillinger, Charles Arthur "Pretty Boy Floyd," George "Machine Gun" Kelly and Baby Face Nelson. These gangsters roamed the country in fast autos, armed with automatic weapons, robbing, kidnapping and often murdering cops and innocents alike. Their bravado and bloody actions mesmerized the public

These dangerous and violent criminals became known as "Public Enemies," a term that became synonymous with "fugitive" and "notorious gangster." The Public Enemies became high profile targets of the FBI and U.S. law enforcement and the subject of many Hollywood movies. The most notable of these flicks, "Public Enemies," which was released in 1931, starred James Cagney and Jean Harlow, and chronicles the story of a young man's rise in the criminal underworld in Prohibition era urban America. Films like "The Public Enemies" became so popular that concerned U.S. government officials created the Haye's Office to censor Hollywood movies.

Most of the Public Enemies were male, but some of them were women, and their criminal exploits became the gist of sensational media stories. The three most famous of the queenpins—Kathryn Kelly, Bonnie Parker and Kate "Ma" Barker—were an unlikely trio, but they became the stuff of American legend.

KATHRYN KELLY WAS most probably the truest queenpin of the three. While historians have generally cast doubt on the nature of the involvement of Bonnie Parker and Ma Barker in actual criminal acts, a close look at the life Katherine Kelly leaves no doubt she was the catalyst and prime mover behind the rise to notoriety of notorious gangster George "Machine Gun" Kelly. Kathryn was a master of public relations and marketing, and through her deft manipulation, George Kelly was built up as a gangster to the point that he became one of the FBI's most targeted criminals. In his 1936 book, *Persons in History*, FBI director J. Edgar Hoover wrote that Kathryn Kelly was one of the most "coldly deliberate criminals of my experience… If there ever was a henpecked husband, it was George (Machine Gun) Kelly."

Kathryn Kelly was born Cleo Brooks in 1904 in Saltillo, Mississippi. By age 15 she was married to a blue collar worker named Lonnie Frye. Yet, from an early age, the young girl aspired to a life of glamour. Kathryn hated her dull life so much that she ditched her lazy husband and started calling herself "Kathryn." By age 20 she was married and divorced again. Unlike George Kelly, her future husband, Kathryn did not come from a well-to-do family. She and various members of her family, in fact, were involved with bootlegging, counterfeiting, prostitution and car theft. In 1929, Kathryn was using the alias Dolores Whitney when Fort Worth, Texas, police charged her with shoplifting. She was also arrested on robbery, prostitution and receipt of stolen property charges.

Kathryn Kelly

Kathryn Kelly was one tough woman. In his book, *Persons in History*, FBI Director J. Edgar Hoover quotes a man who recalled for him what happened when he dated Kathryn Kelly. "Remember than innocent little girl I was going to show a good time? She took me to more speakeasies, more bootleg dives, more holes in the wall than I thought there were in all of Texas... She can drink liquor like water. And she's got some of the toughest women friends I ever laid eyes on."

Kathryn got involved in the bootlegging business when she married bootlegger Charlie Thorne. Unlike her previous marriage, however, she did not divorce him. Thorne was found shot to death. Although a coroner ruled his death a suicide, suspicion fell on Kathryn, who allegedly told a gas station attendant the day before her husband's death that "I'm bound for Coleman, Texas, to kill that goddamn Charlie Thorne." No one was ever convicted, let alone arrested for Thorne's murder.

In early 1930, after having served three years in Leavenworth Penitentiary and another stretch in the New Mexico State

Penitentiary, George Kelly hooked up with Kathryn and her boyfriend, Steve Anderson, a small-time bootlegger. George fell hard for Kathryn and they soon became inseparable. Legend has it that George and Kathryn stole Anderson's sixteen cylinder Cadillac and prize-winning English bulldog when they ran off to be married in September 1930.

GEORGE, WHO WAS born George Kelly Barnes, was the son of an insurance executive and had opportunities to do something with his life. George even enrolled at Mississippi A & M University (later Mississippi State University) in Jackson to study agriculture, but he did poorly in school and dropped out in January 1918. The young man seemed intent on being a criminal, but he still had the presence of mine to change his name to George Kelly to protect his family's good name when he began his life of crime. Later George would tell Alcatraz Penitentiary warden James A. Johnston: "My family are good people. Only I turned out to be a heel."

By all accounts young George was a nondescript character. In his best selling book, Public Enemies, Bryan Burrough wrote that "the most impressive thing about (George) Kelly remains his nickname." Burrough explained: "He was never the menacing figure his moniker suggests. He was glib, a dreamer and a joker, the kind of man who said things like, "Working hard or hardly working."

But when Kathryn purchased her husband's first machine gun, the myth of Machine Gun Kelly was born. George had been a small-time gangster, but under Kathryn's influence, he was catapulted into the status of a Public Enemy Number 1. She did her best to promote her husband's name in public and in the criminal underworld. Some historians even believe she coined her husband's nickname of "Machine Gun." Among other initiatives, Kathryn was known to take spent gun cartridges and pass them around to people in the underground drinking establishments, explaining that they were souvenirs from her husband, "Machine Gun" Kelly. Kathryn's campaign worked. By August 1933, the FBI had published wanted posters describing Kelly as an "expert machine gunner."

It is also believed that Kathryn masterminded some of the George's crimes. "It's unlikely he would have risen to prominence if not for his wife, Kathryn, a sly blond whom J. Edgar Hoover would repeatedly demonize in press accounts," Burroughs wrote. In his memoir, Hoover wrote that Kathryn was "man crazy," "cloths crazy" and "a cunning, shrewd criminal actress."

IN PARTNERSHIP WITH a variety of gangsters, George and Kathryn embarked on a bank robbery and kidnapping spree that propelled them to national attention. On July 15, 1930, George helped rob the Bank of Willmar in Willmar, Minnesota of $70,000. On April 8, 1931, another robbery netted the pair $40,000. On January 27, 1932, George collaborated on his first kidnapping: Howard Woolverton, a local manufacturer and baker's son from South Bend, Indiana. Woolverton was driven around northern Indiana for two days before he convinced George and an accomplice that it would take time to raise the $50,000 the kidnappers demanded, but he could be counted on to come through with the payment.

Not the swiftest of gangsters, George released Woolverton on the basis of the promise. Woolverton never kept his promise and simply ignored the threatening letters and phone call from his kidnappers that demanded: Pay up or else!

Machine Gun Kelly still thought he had a criminal future in kidnapping, but because of his incompetence, his next attempt proved to be as disastrous as his first. On July 22, 1933, George and his accomplice entered the front porch of the Oklahoma City mansion of Charles Urschel, an oil tycoon from one of Oklahoma's wealthiest citizens, and encountered two couples playing bridge. "Which one of you is Urschel?" the kidnappers demanded. When no one answered, the kidnappers took the two men with them. They drove outside the city before they were able to identify Urschel. They let the other man go and drove Urschel to a ranch in Texas. Meanwhile, Urschel's wife notified the local police and the FBI.

Several days went by before Mrs. Urschel and two family friends were able to raise the $200,000 ransom. After they delivered the money on July 30, Urschel was released the following night near Norman, Oklahoma, where he walked to a barbecue stand and called a taxi.

Urschel was a sharp man and he was able to remember many details about his kidnapping. He was blindfolded but managed to count his footsteps to various places where he was hidden and made a mental note of audible sounds. Moreover, he left his fingerprints everywhere. When the authorities raided the ranch where Urschel was held, they discovered that George Kelly was the mastermind of the Urschel kidnapping.

A national manhunt got underway for the Kellys as the couple moved to stay one step ahead of the law. They dyed their hair to conceal their identity but still managed to live a lavish lifestyle, not the best of moves for two high profile gangsters on the run. The FBI tracked the Kellys to Memphis, Tennessee, and in the early morning hours of September 26, 1933, they were captured and taken into custody. Caught by surprise and without a weapon, George was reported to have cried out as he surrendered: "Don't shoot, G-Men. Don't shoot, G-Men!" Ever since, the term G-Man has become synonymous with FBI agents.

The takedown of the Kelly gang marked a turning point in the FBI's history. It was one thing to have a list of public enemies; it was another to follow through and capture them.

During the trial, Kathryn denied having anything to do with the Urschel kidnapping or with any other crimes, for that matter. Kathryn's father testified in her defense, claiming, "She was never in any trouble as far as I knew until she met (George Kelly). Kelly was her downfall. You know a woman usually does whatever husband says."

On October 23, 1933, the Kellys were sentenced to life in prison. George was sent to Leavenworth and Kathryn to a federal prison in Cincinnati. Kathryn told the press that she still loved George, and when he vowed to escape by Christmas, Kathryn proclaimed her faith in her husband.

"George will see me by Christmas," Kathryn predicted. "He told me he would break out by Christmas and get me out. He always does as he says he will."

But the great breakout did not happen. Instead, George rotted away in prison. He dropped dead of a heart attack on July 17, 1958, in Leavenworth. Over the years, Kathryn had constantly petitioned J. Edgar Hoover for her release, but the petitions were turned down.

Finally, Kathryn convinced a judge to give her a new trial. Caught off guard, the FBI scrambled to reassemble its case against Kathryn, but the trial had taken place 25 years ago and the Bureau could not re-produce the evidence in time to get her convicted again. Kathryn was finally released from prison. She moved to Oklahoma, where she worked in a hospital for several years before dying in obscurity in 1985.

AT THE TIME the Kellys were sentenced to life in prison, another notorious pair of lovers were also trying to survive. Bonnie Parker and Clyde Barrow became more famous than the Kellys, and they left a violent and bloody trail of robbery and murder across Texas, Oklahoma, Missouri and New Mexico.

Bonnie Elizabeth Parker was the most unlikely candidate for legendary queenpin status. Nothing in her early background indicted that she would grow up to be a famous gangster. Born On October 1, 1910, in Rowena, Kansas, the blonde, blue eyed young girl was not only good looking but also articulate, witty, charming and popular. She was close to her mother, attended Baptist church every Sunday and, despite the poverty of her youth, was a good student with an aptitude for creative writing. Bonnie dreamed of growing up to be someone special—a singer, an actress or a poet perhaps. As John Neal Phillips wrote in his book *Running with Bonnie and Clyde*, "Bonnie had been immensely popular in school and throughout her years as a waitress in three downtown restaurants. There was hardly a businessman, county official or a lawman who didn't know or liked her." But Phillips also noted, "Despite her ability with people... Bonnie felt inferior."

Bonnie lacked good judgment as well, evident in her choice of boyfriends. She seemed to gravitate to boys who were bad to the bone. At age 16, Bonnie married Roy Thornton, a loser of whom her mother did not approve. Bonnie quit school and she seemed content to be Roy's devoted wife, but within a few months, Roy was thrown in jail, and she needed to work to support herself. When she took a job as waitress, it looked to Bonnie as if her life had reached rock bottom.

BUT IN DECEMBER 1929, Bonnie was swept off her feet by Clyde Chestnut Barrow, a 21-year slightly built, 5, 7", innocent looking petty criminal. Indeed, it was love at first sight. The romance became legendary in March 1930 when Clyde escaped from jail with the help of a gun that Bonnie smuggled into the prison. Clyde, however, was captured the next month and sent to a prison farm in Crockett, Texas. When paroled in February 1932, Clyde took up with Bonnie again. They would remain inseparable the rest of their short lives, as they pursued their notorious course as public enemies. The couple fueled the legend by using a camera to take photos of themselves as they traveled and committed crimes, often leaving some of them behind when they fled.

The seemingly passionate love affair was remarkable given that Clyde reportedly had sexual problems, the result, it is believed, from the sexual abuse he suffered during his incarceration in Eastham Prison Farm near Huntsville, Texas, beginning in April 1930. Being young and "pretty," Clyde became a "bitch" for an inmate named Ed Crowder, who reportedly raped and beat Clyde. Fed up with the abuse, Clyde lured the much bigger Crowder into a bathroom where he beat him to death with a lead pipe. It was Clyde's first killing, but it would not be his last. Leaving prison, Clyde was a hardened and violence prone criminal.

Some historians have questioned the extent of Bonnie's role in Clyde's crimes and whether she even fired a gun. Some of the gangsters who operated with Bonnie and Clyde said that they never saw Bonnie fire a gun, but they are often inconsistent in

Bonnie and Clyde

their recollections. For instance, in 1933, while being questioned by authorities, W. D. James first recalled that Bonnie fired a gun at police officers "two or three times."

By 1968 his recollection had changed. He now said: "During the five big gun battles I was with them, she (Bonnie) never fired a gun." But James added: "...I'll say she was one hell of a loader."

Marie, Clyde Barrow's youngest sister, also said essentially the same thing. "Bonnie never fired a shot. She just followed my brother, no matter where he went."

We will never know Bonnie's true role in the Bonnie and Clyde legend. Yet, there is no doubt Bonnie wanted to be with Clyde while he was on the run. He was the love of her young life and she did not want be with anyone else.

Their violent crime-ridden story made them antiheroes, and they had a lot of public support. After all, it was the Depression, and the banks they robbed stood as the symbol of what had gone wrong with the average American's life. The banks had not only foreclosed on people's homes but on their American Dream as well. Bonnie and Clyde were thumbing their noses at the corrupt status quo, something many Americans, themselves, wanted to do.

Yet, despite their fame, Bonnie and Clyde were really small-time hoods who mainly robbed grocery stores and small banks. They didn't plan their moves but simply robbed whatever establishment was convenient when they ran out of money. A robbery of $2,000 was a large haul for them.

As law enforcement intensified their hunt for the young lovers, Bonnie and Clyde had no illusion about their ultimate fate. According to writer E.L. Milner, the author of *The Lives and Times of Bonnie and Clyde*, "The two recognized that their deaths were inevitable. They simply hoped to delay the inevitable for as long as possible and remain free on a sort of apocryphal appeal."

Bonnie wrote her mother a poem titled: "The Story of Bonnie and Clyde," which foreshadowed their fate. It began:

> *You've heard the story of Jesse James*
> *Of how they lived and died*
> *If you're still in need of something to read*
> *Here is the story of Bonnie and Clyde.*

The poem went on for 15 stanzas, ending with:

> *Some day they will go down together*
> *And they'll bury them side by side*
> *To few it will be grief, to the law a relief*
> *But it's death for Bonnie and Clyde.*

YET, FOR A time, fate seemed to be with the young gangsters. In March 1932, authorities captured Bonnie in a foiled robbery attempt and jailed her in Kauffman, Texas. When the grand jury met in June 1932, Bonnie was no-billed and released. Within a few weeks, she was back with Clyde, and the duo then embarked on a nihilistic murder spree across the Midwest and Southwest.

Bonnie and Clyde lived as if there was no tomorrow. Somehow, they survived several narrow escapes, including a police raid on their hideout in Joplin, Missouri, where they made a dramatic escape while gunning down two policemen. On one occasion near Wellington, Texas, Clyde was driving so fast and recklessly that he drove the car off a washed out bridge. Clyde escaped without injury, but Bonnie got trapped in the car. She was severely burned, and the ordeal became so painful for her that she begged Clyde to kill her. Instead, Clyde managed to get Bonnie out of the car and to a nearby farm where he coerced the owners to help care for Bonnie. She recovered but walked with a limp the rest of her life.

FROM THE TIME Clyde was paroled from prison in 1933 and rejoined Bonnie to the time the FBI caught up with them, it is believed that Bonnie and Clyde committed 13 murders. On April 30, 1932, during as robbery of a grocery store, a gun went off and the grocery store owner was killed. Near Alma, Arkansas, the two murdered the town marshal. In January 1933 they killed a guard while helping their friend Raymond Hamilton escape from Eastham Prison Farm.

On Eastern Sunday, 1934, near Grapevine, Texas, Bonnie and Clyde shocked the nation with their most brazen killing. They parked their Ford automobile alongside the highway near Grapevine, Texas and began to have good time, laughing, talking and throwing whisky bottles out the windows. H.D. Murphy and Edward Bryant Wheeler, two highway patrolmen came by on motorcycles and stopped to check on what they thought was a stalled vehicle. It is not clear who fired first, but when the officers came up to the car, both were shot dead.

One popular account has Bonnie walking up to one of the officers, rolling him over with one foot and using a sawed off shotgun to shoot him point blank in the head as she exclaimed: "Look-a-there, his head bounced just like a rubber ball."

But another account has Bonnie sleeping in the Ford's backseat while the shoot out occurred. Less than a week later, Bonnie and Clyde committed their last murder when they blew away a police officer in Commerce, Oklahoma.

Killing the police officers galvanized the authorities, and hundreds of law enforcement officers mobilized to hunt for Bonnie and Clyde. The authorities learned that Bonnie, Clyde and some of their associates in crime had held a party at their hideout at Black Lake, Louisiana, and that they were to return to the area in two days. The beginning of the end for Bonnie and Clyde came on May 23, 1934, on a desolate Louisiana highway. A posse composed of police officers from Louisiana and Texas concealed themselves in bushes along the highway and waited. The next day, just after dawn, the posse spotted a Ford that fit the description of an auto Clyde had stolen in Topeka, Kansas. The car was moving fast at high speed and it was being driven in a manner familiar with Clyde Barrow.

The police recognized Bonnie and Clyde, but Clyde also spotted the police and grabbed his gun. The police opened up on the Ford with a barrage of from 130 to 167 bullets. When the lawmen stopped firing, they moved cautiously to inspect the bullet-ridden auto. Inside, they found Bonnie, her 90-pound frame riddled with at least 28 bullets, her jaw shattered, teeth crushed and several fingers torn from her right hand by gun fire. Bonnie Parker was dead at 23.

The bodies of Bonnie and Clyde were taken to Dallas, Texas, for burial. The lovers had wanted to be buried side by side, but the Parker family would not allow it. Pandemonium reigned at Bonnie's gravesite in Crown Hill Memorial Park. With more than 20,000 people turning out for Bonnie's funeral, it was difficult for her family to reach the grave.

Today, visitors to the cemetery can see Bonnie's tombstone. It is engraved with the words:

> *All the flowers are all made sweeter: by the sunshine and the dew.*
> *So this old world is made brighter: by the lives of folks like you.*

THE PUBLIC ENEMIES era did not end with the deaths of Bonnie and Clyde, or those of the other legendary gangsters of the era, John Dillinger, Charles Arthur "Pretty Boy" Floyd and Lester Joseph Gillis aka George "Baby Face" Nelson. One of the most gangs still on the loose included a mother and her four sons, who, together, comprised one of the most notorious crime families in U.S. history.

The mother and queenpin was Kate "Ma" Barker and her role in the Barker gang's criminal activities has been controversial ever since the mid 1930s. Many believe Ma Barker played little or no actual role in the gang's criminality. One associate of the Barker family, Harvey Bailey, told L.L. Edge, the author of *Run the Cat Roads* that: "Ma couldn't plan breakfast. When we got down to plan a bank robbery, she'd go into the other room and listen to Amos and Andy or hillbilly music on the radio."

In the 1971 autobiography, *The Alvin Karpis Story*, which Alvin Karpis penned with Bill Trent, Karpis, who worked closely with Ma Barker's son, Fred, claimed that: "The most ridiculous story in the annals of crime is that Ma Barker was the mastermind... She wasn't a leader of criminals or even a criminal herself. There is not one police photograph for her or a set of finger prints taken while she was alive. She knew we were criminals, but her participation in our crimes was limited to one function. When we were together, we moved as a mother and her sons. What could look more innocent?"

It's also true, however, that Kate Barker was a mother who believed her sons could do no wrong and that, without her gross parental indulgence, the sons might not have turned into the violent and dangerous criminals they became. She was blindly dedicated to her sons to the point that, whenever her sons got into trouble, she would claim it was the authorities fault. She saw her four sons not as delinquents who needed to be punished so they would be deterred from getting into further trouble, but as victims of the police. As her sons grew up, she would rather move her family than deal with the consequences of her four son's criminal actions. Ma Barker truly let them get away with murder, and, intentional or not, she helped steer her sons on to the crooked path.

KATE "MA" BARKER was born Arizona Donna Clark in 1872 or 1873 on a small farm near Springfield, Missouri, in the poor hillbilly country of the Ozark Mountains Her nicknamed was "Arrie." It was later said that Ma could remember the famous outlaw Jesse James riding through her town one day and that the event made a memorable impression on her.

Ma was a head strung young girl, plumb, with dark penetrating eyes and a bad temper. She attended church regularly and sang in the choir. In 1892 Ma married soft spoken laid back tenant farmer George Barker, who was 13 years her senior. It was not a move out of poverty for Ma, but she was seemingly blessed with the birth of four sons between 1893 and 1902: Herman, Lloyd, Arthur "Dock" and Fred. The four kids grew up in an impoverished tar paper shack to become a crew of pint sized trouble makers who were frequently absent from school, got into fights with other kids and shoplifted from the local stores.

George left the child rearing to his wife who spoiled them rotten. Whenever the boys got into trouble, Ma cajoled the authorities into releasing them. She called anyone who complained about her sons a liar and would tell them to get lost. Ma was almost paranoid in her belief that society was out to get her sons. She was even extremely jealous of her sons' girl friends. The boys knew better than to introduce their girlfriends to their mother, and they didn't.

Yet, the Barker boys were, no doubt, devoted to their mother. Insight into the bond between Ma and sons was evident when, while the Barker gang was on the run, the police found a large trunk containing photos and letters, several of which were exchanged between Ma and her sons. According to author Robert Winter, "The letters between Kate and her sons showed an unusual strong bond between them. They (the boys) poured out their love and confidence in her (Ma). Many (letters) expressed the belief she would stand by them to the death."

As they grew up, the Barker boys gravitated to more serious crimes, and by 1923 all of them were in jail or in reformatories. In 1916 Herman was sentenced to 10 years in jail for larceny and burglary. In 1926 Fred got a five- to ten-year prison sentence. The following year, Herman killed himself when cornered by police in Wichita, Kansas. In 1928 Lloyd began serving 25-years in Leavenworth for mail robbery. Four years later, Oklahoma governor William "Alfalfa" Murray pardoned Dock from his life sentence for the murder of a security guard, but several crime historians believe Dock was released because he was able to bribe his way out of prison.

By 1927, George Barker left his family, realizing that he would never have any control over his delinquent sons. Later George would say: "She would never let me do with them what I wanted to do."

Ma Barker

THE BARKERS FORTUNES

began to change in 1932 when Fred hooked up with career criminal Alvin Karpis whom he had met in 1930 while in prison. They had decided that, upon their release, they would hook up and plan crimes that would bring them big money. When Dock was released the following year, the notorious Barker-Karpis gang was born. Ma Barker embraced Alvin Karpis like a son, but Karpis would later describe Ma as resembling "a slightly nutty old woman."

The Barker-Karpis gang began a crime spree in which they robbed several banks across the Midwest. On March 29, 1932, the gang robbed a bank in Memphis, Tennessee, hauling in $250,000 in cash and bonds, the equivalent in today's money of $3 million. Ma Barker was no longer a poor hillbilly mother from the Ozarks, and her lifestyle changed. According to one FBI report, "Ma Barker liked to live well. She purchased expensive clothing, furniture and other necessities from the spoils of her sons' depredation."

While the gang kept on the move to stay ahead of the law, Ma Barker posed as a mother traveling with her children. She would be overjoyed when the boys returned from crime job and greet them with a home cooked meal.

Meanwhile, the murders mounted. The Barker-Karpis gang did not hesitate to kill anyone who got in their way, even innocent victims. After George Barker walked out on his family, Ma Barker too up with an Arthur Dunlap, who was known to be lazy and shiftless. Dunlap's body was found riddled with bullets and dumped in a Minnesota hole after the gang suspected that Dunlap was talking too much and may have inadvertently tipped off the cops to one of their hideouts. George Zeigler was a member of the gang, but that did not stop the gang from murdering him as well in Cicero, Illinois.

On November 8, 1931, the gang murdered Pocahontas, Missouri, police chief Manley Jackson. The following month, they blew away Sheriff C. Roy Kelley in Monett, Missouri, when he entered a garage on East Main Street. He wanted to question three men in a blue De Soto who were having two tires repaired. When the sheriff opened the car door, shots rang out and Sheriff Kelley fell dead. Tires screeched and the blue De Soto was gone.

In the ensuing manhunt, the De Soto was found. In checking the license plate, the police learned that the car belonged to an Alvin Karpis, a member of Barker-Karpis gang. The police investigation led them to a farm that they discovered was rented by a Mr. and Mrs. Arthur Dunlap of Oklahoma. Further digging revealed that Mrs. Arthur Dunlap was, in actuality, Kate Barker and that the Barker-Karpis gang was using the farmhouse as a hideout.

THE GANG HIT financial pay dirt with two high profile kidnappings in St. Paul, Minnesota, at separate apartments located within four blocks of each other. In 1933 the gang kidnapped William Hamm, a wealthy Minnesota brewer of Hamm's beer, and ransomed him for $100,000. The FBIs investigation of the kidnapping became its first attempt to identify latent fingerprints from paper ransom notes. The family paid the ransom, and the kidnappers released Hamm unharmed in Wyoming, Minnesota.

The second kidnapping victim was Edward George Bremer, a bank executive and son of Adolph Bremer, part owner of the Jacob Schmidt Brewing Company. The kidnapping happened in January 1934, just after Bremer had dropped his daughter off at school. The Barker-Karpis gang upped the ransom demand for Bremer's release to $200,000. When the ransom was paid in February 1934, the kidnappers released Bremer unharmed.

After Bremer's kidnapping, the gang was put on the FBI's Public Enemies list, and the law enforcement pressure on the gang intensified. The Barker gang became the Bureau's number one target after other high profile gangsters on the list—John Dellinger, Baby Face Nelson and Pretty Boy Floyd—were gunned down and eliminated. The FBI zeroed in on the gang. It would be just a matter of time before the Feds would catch up with it.

Inside Dock's apartment, the Feds found a map with the town of Ocala circled. Dock kept his mouth shut, but Byron Bolton, another Barker-Karpis member, who was also arrested in January, agreed to snitch in return for a reduced sentence. Bolton told the authorities that Ma Barker, son Fred and possibly other gang members were living on a lake in Florida, where Fred, who was obsessed with using a submachine gun hunted a huge alligator that locals had nicknamed Joe.

On January 16, 1935, a small army of federal agents descended on a two-story house on Lake Weir, Kalawao. After the houses occupants failed to heed the FBI's call to surrender, a blazing gun battle ensued in which the G-men pumped about 1,500 rounds into the house. The army found Ma and son Fred

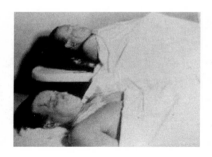

Ma and Fred lay side by side in morgue

dead in an upstairs bedroom. Fred had 14 bullets in him. Nearby, lay his mother, dead from a single gunshot wound, which may or may not have been self-inflicted, or perhaps Fred had fired the bullet as capture seemed imminent. We will never know for sure.

Until the shootout, The Barker-Karpis gang had received a mere fraction of the publicity that the other gangsters on FBI's Public Enemies list had received, Killing Ma Barker embarrassed the Bureau. She was not yet buried when the FBI began manufacturing her legend. The weapons confiscated at the scene of the shootout were not dusted for prints, and so it is unclear if Ma was actually shooting a gun when she was killed. So J. Edgar Hoover, the Bureaus Director, fed the newspapers the story that Ma Barker had died while armed with a Thompson submachine gun. In 1938 Hoover wrote: "The most vicious, dangerous and resourceful criminal brain this country has produced in many years belongs to a person called Mother Barker. To her (her sons) looked for guidance, for daring, for resourcefulness. They obeyed her implicitly."

Since the mid 1930s, the deaths of the three queenpins— Kathryn Kelly, Bonnie Parker and Ma Barker—have inspired books, music, movies and TV shows. In 1960, actress Laurene Tuttle portrayed Ma Barker in a low-budget feature film. Ten years later, horror filmmaker Roger Corman directed "Bloody Mama," a film starring Shelley Winters as the mother of Fred, who was played by a young actor named Robert De Niro. The movie depicts a corrupt mother who encourages and directs her sons' criminality. Meanwhile, in 1977, the musical group Boney M. released a single record titled "Mother" that added to legend of Ma Barker. Indeed, time has only enhanced Ma Barkers stature as a queenpin.

America, it seems, loves anti heroes and none more so than Bonnie and Clyde. Remarkably, a Clyde Barrow family member was able to sell the bloody shirt that Clyde wore the day he died at auction for $85,000. Clyde's pants were even cut into pieces and sold as well. The 1967 movie, "Bonnie and Clyde," starring Fay Dunaway and Warren Beatty as Bonnie and Clyde, was a hit. Their short violent story has also inspired half a dozen songs, from Merle Haggard's "The Legend of Bonnie and Clyde" to Jay-Z's "03 Bonnie & Clyde."

Popular culture has immortalized Kathryn and George "Machine Gun" Kelly as well. For example, in the 1958 film, "Machine-Gun Kelly," which starred Charles Bronson, Kelly's crimes are loosely portrayed. Machine Gun Kelly is also the central character in the 1974 film, "Melvin Purvis-G-Man."

The lives of the Queenpins and the central characters in their lives were brief. Bad choices doomed them to either too long prison terms or death. Still, the queenpins live on as notorious legends of gangland.

FIVE

Mob Queen

DURING THE LATER years of Prohibition, Machine Gun and Kathryn Kelly, the Ma Barker gang, Bonnie and Clyde and the other Public Enemies captured America's attention as some of the country's most famous gangsters. By the mid 1930s, however, a far more powerful and sinister criminal force took root in the country. The Italian American Mafia, or La Cosa Nostra, exploded on the American scene in 1920 with the introduction of Prohibition, a movement that gave the Mob the opportunity to develop into a sophisticated criminal enterprise skilled at smuggling, bribery and money laundering. By the 1920s a power struggle known as the Castellammarese War broke out between the New York City Mob's two biggest gangs. Salvatore Maranzano came out on top on April 15, 1931, when he had his bitter rival, Joe Masseria, killed at a restaurant in Brooklyn's Coney Island.

But in an act of treachery typical in the Mob underworld, Maranzano, himself, was murdered six months later by four hit men dressed as police men. Charles "Lucky" Luciano and Vito Genovese, two powerful mobsters who came to play a prominent role in the American Mafia during the coming decades, orchestrated the hit. Luciano became the Godfather of the New York Mob, and he set up a ruling commission that included bosses from the Mafia's five leading crime families.

Meanwhile, another powerful Mafia, known as The Outfit, had organized in Chicago, and it continued to rule organized crime in the Windy City long after Prohibition ended in 1933. Al "Scarface" Capone emerged as Chicago's most powerful mobster after a vicious gang war that resulted in hundreds of murders. Two years later, an IRS investigation caused Capone's removal from the Chicago crime scene, for he was convicted of tax evasion and slapped with an 11-year prison sentence. Mobster Paul Ricca grabbed power from Frank Nitti, Capone's handpicked successor, and after Prohibition Ricca led The Outfit into labor racketeering, gambling and loan sharking, activities that helped spread the Mob's criminal influence as far as Hollywood, where its extortion of labor unions gave it leverage over the film industry.

BOTH THE CHICAGO and New York City Mafias were male dominated and their godfathers expected their women to stay in the background and out of their business. In the mid 1930s, however, an unusual teenager appeared on the Chicago Mob scene, and she emerged as the most powerful woman in American Mafia history. Virginia Hill was beautiful, smart, cunning, foul mouthed and knew how to seize opportunity for her advantage. From the 1930s through the 1950s, she worked as a Mob courier and one of its top money launderers, who in her "business" travels had countless affairs with many powerful godfathers, including Benjamin Siegel, Joe Adonis and Frank Costello in New York City and Moe Dalitz of Detroit and Tony Accardo in Chicago.

As a courier for The Outfit, Hill was able to spy on the activities of its organized crime partners around the country, and she became privy to the machinations and inner workings of The Outfit. As author Andy Edmonds explained in her biography of Hill, *Bugsy Baby,* Hill was: "One of the few women ever allowed to sit at the table with gang leaders when

Virginia Hill

they mapped out plans for takeovers, hits and business ventures. For much of her life, Virginia Hill had the Mafia's trust and learned its darkest secrets."

Jack Dragna, a powerful Mobster in Hollywood, said of Hill: "She was the only woman who could be trusted to keep her mouth shut."

Hill knew the power her beauty and sexual attraction held over the opposite sex and she was not shy about letting the public know it. That included the members of the powerful Senate Special Committee to Investigate Organized Crime in Interstate Gambling. Hill questioned in 1952 by committee member Senator Charles Tobey about why a mobster would give her so much money to handle.

"You really want to know?" Hill asked.

"Yes, I really want to know," pressed Senator Tobey.

"Then I will tell you why," Virginia said. "Because I'm the best cocksucker in town!"

NOTHING THAT HAPPENED in Virginia Hill's formative years foreshadowed the fame and fortune she would gain as a Mob Queen. She was born on August 26, 1916, in Lipscomb,

Alabama, the seventh of ten children of W.M. "Mack" Hill, a livery and stable operator and horse and mule trader. Mac was a drunk who loved to abuse his wife and children. When Virginia was around seven years old, she had had enough of the abuse and, one evening, clobbered her father with an iron skillet still sizzling with grease. Mack never touched his daughter again.

Virginia dropped out of school in the eighth grade, but from an early age made up for her lack of formal education with street smarts. By age 12, the young girl had already blossomed into a buxom, sexy, sultry young girl who attracted the attention of the boys in Lipscomb.

As Edmonds explained, "Even as a young girl, sex to Virginia was nothing more than a means to achieving her goals—money and notoriety."

Later, Virginia admitted that she rarely turned down a boy who asked her for sex.

As a teenager, Virginia found life in small town Alabama dull and boring. She yearned for the life of the big city that she had read about in books and heard about in conversations around town. In August 1933, Virginia made her move, leaving the rural South to find work in Chicago at the Century of Progress Exhibition, which was attracting tourists from all over the country.

Although the record is sketchy, it appeared that Virginia found work at the San Carlo Italian Village restaurant, an establishment frequented by members of Chicago's Outfit. Virginia made the most of the opportunities that contact with Mob figures at the restaurant generated. At one of the parties she attended, Virginia caught the attention of Mobster Joe Epstein, the powerful overseer of The Outfit's Chicago-area horse racing, wire services and other gambling operations. Epstein's operation was hugely successful, as some of his bookmakers hauled in thousands of dollars daily. Epstein was educated, an intellectual by underworld standards, but he liked to party as much as Virginia did.

That was about all they had in common. In contrast to Epstein who was urbane and mild mannered, Virginia was hot tempered, volatile and rough around the edges. Virginia became known in the underworld as "Epstein's girl," but rumors swirled that Epstein was gay, a lifestyle, if proven to be true, would have put him in a delicate position with the Mob. So being seen with a beautiful and sexy woman did not hurt his image.

"Virginia helped Epstein put on a more socially acceptable front," said Edmonds. "It explained why Epstein always remained at Hill's side during her numerous love affairs and even promoted her sexual encounters with others connected to the underworld."

Epstein was Virginia's entry into the Mafia and he changed her life. He furnished Virginia with the finest cloths, polished her look and helped her lose the white trash image. Epstein saw Virginia as a talent, and he began to train her for a Mob role. He started by letting the teenager make small wagers at the race track around Chicago and Indiana and then taught her how to operate as a money launderer and transporter of stolen property across state line into Indiana and Michigan and sometimes as far away as Miami. Eventually some of the cash shipments that Virginia made for Epstein were worth more than $10,000.

BY 1956, VIRGINIA'S sexual exploits had earned her a reputation, deservedly or not, as a Mob slut who would spread her legs for any mobster whom she thought could help her get ahead in life. The Mobsters' wives hated Virginia and didn't trust her to be with their husbands. The wives were right to be distrustful, given Virginia's seemingly insatiable sexual appetite, but their hatred of the budding Mob Queen did not deter her.

At one Mob party in December 1936, to which Virginia attended with Epstein, she came on strong to every mobster present, regardless of whether the mobster was with his wife or not. Before too long, some of the mobsters challenged Virginia to put her mouth where the money was. Virginia got on her hands and knees performing fellatio on every man in the room. The wives were outraged and called Virginia a "whore." Virginia smirked and ignored the insult.

Little did the panting mobsters or their outraged wives know that she was secretly collecting incriminating evidence and recording it in a secret diary, which, if made public, could have destroyed The Outfit. Later, she collected information on such heavyweights of the Mob world as Meyer Lansky and Frank Costello.

Born in 1891, Frank Costello, a boyhood friend of Luciano who was known as the "Prime Minister of the Underworld," rose to the top of La Cosa Nostra and oversaw a vast gambling empire extending across the U.S. About 1937, Costello became head of the Luciano crime family after Lucky was convicted of running a prostitution ring and received a long prison sentence. Lucky's chosen successor, Vito Genovese, fled to Naples, Italy, after being indicted for murder in 1937.

Born of Jewish parents the same year as Costello, Lansky was known as "The Brain" because of his criminal brilliance. He was another close associate of Luciano and became one of the highest ranking members of La Cosa Nostra, even though he was not Italian. By the time Virginia moved to New York City, Lansky had established gambling operations for the Mob in Florida, New York City and Cuba. The bold act of keeping written tabs on such powerful men showed that Virginia had plenty of old fashioned cahones because it would have been a death sentence for her if the Mob found out what she was doing.

THE CHICAGO MOB gave Virginia increasing responsibilities, eventually sending her to New York City, ostensibly to act as a liaison with the New York City based La Cosa Nostra, then under the leadership of Godfather Lucky Luciano. In reality, she was a spy whose job was to infiltrate the inner circle of the New York Mob. Meanwhile, she began transporting stolen property between New York and Chicago for Moe Dalitz in Detroit, Joe Adonis and Tony Accardo in Chicago, Epstein and Charles Fischetti in Chicago and Johnny Roselli in Hollywood.

To do her assignment for The Outfit, Virginia slept with some of the most powerful mobsters in New York City. At the head of the line was Joe Adonis, who became Joey A. in Virginia's diary. Born in 1902, in a small town near Naples Italy, Adonis had stowed away on an ocean liner bound for New York City and settled in Brooklyn. By the time Virginia met Joey A, he had risen through the ranks of the New York mafia and was playing an important part in its development. Adonis was a member of the Mob's National Commission and had many important politicians and well placed police officers on his payroll. Virginia played her spy role so well that she began working for Adonis in much the same way she had for Epstein.

Virginia's relationship with Joey A did not deter her from having sexual trysts with other mobsters. In 1937, while on the arm of Adonis, Virginia met the Hollywood handsome Benjamin Siegel at a Brooklyn bar. Born on February 28, 1906, in New York City, Bugsy Siegel grew up a small tenement house as one of five children of Jewish-Austrian parents. Young Benjamin shunned school and turned to the streets where, by age 19, he was a petty criminal running craps games. His life changed when he met and befriended Meyer Lansky and they started a gang. By this time, Benjamin had earned the reputation of being "crazier than a bug," and he became known as "Bugsy" Siegel. The budding gangster grew up to be a bully and a ruthless thug who would go ballistic to the point where it would be impossible to calm him down.

Tony Stipone told author Andy Edmonds what happened the time Bugsy used his signature trademark on a gangster who tried to cheat him in a poker game: "The stiff drops to the floor and Benny's (Bugsy) watching the dead guy twist and jerk on the floor, how dead guys do, telling the two of us to watch the bum dance. When the guy quit movin', Ben lifts him upon and perches the dead guy back in the chair. He deals again. We all ante up."

By the time Bugsy met Virginia Hill, he was a member of the Mob's Murder Inc. and one of the top hit men in New York City. Bugsy may have been crazier than a bug, but he was also charming when he wanted something, especially from the point of view of the opposite sex. Indeed, Bugsy was as sex obsessed as Virginia, and at their first encounter at the Brooklyn bar, the sparks flew. Virginia would later confide that Bugsy was the best sex partner she ever had. Still, despite the mutual attraction, neither lover was faithful to the other.

Virginia was actually taking a chance being with Bugsy. After all, she was an employee of the Chicago Outfit and spending the night with the handsome gangster from a rival Mob was akin to sleeping with the enemy. The penalty for such an indiscretion could have been death. Yet, Virginia got away with it, probably because it was just a one night stand. Virginia and Bugsy would not see each other again for another two years.

WHEN BUGSY'S BOSS, Lucky Luciano, was arrested for extorting prostitutes, Bugsy worried that the law might be getting too close to him, too. So with the Mob's approval, he left New York City for sunny Hollywood, where he oversaw gambling, race track and book making rackets on the West Coast.

In May 1938, Virginia felt she needed a break, too, and moved home to Marietta, Georgia. She was just 23 years old, but it seemed she had already lived a lifetime. While Virginia rose in the Mob ranks, she was good to her family, sending money that helped them move into a better home.

It took just two months at Marietta, though, before Virginia was itching to get back into the action. She took her brother Chick and left Georgia in July bound for the West Coast. Arriving in Hollywood in late August 1938, it was not long before Virginia was making the local news as the sexy woman about Tinsel Town who carried a big wad of dough.

Her brief fling with heart throb actor Errol Flynn became an item after the local newspapers and movie industry trade magazine reported on their drunken brawl. In January 1940, the Mob Queen was still pursuing her career as money launderer and smuggler when she suddenly married to Miguelito Carlos Gonzalez Valdes in a ploy to get Valdes legally into the U.S. The marriage did not last long, but, by now, Virginia was a big-enough celebrity in Hollywood that local gossip columnists noted the break up.

MEANWHILE, BUGSY WAS becoming one of the most powerful and well-known mobsters in Hollywood, hanging with such famous movie stars as George Raft, Jean Harlow, Clark

Bugsy Siegel

Gable, Mae West and Al Jolson, and throwing lavish parties that often turned into orgies. Always taken with himself, Bugsy believed that in another time he could have been a movie star. Rumors even circulated about how the mobster had taken a screen test.

Virginia was also enamored with the movies and she landed some minor roles in several films. On the set of one film, she became acquainted with George Raft, the film's star.

Bugsy would brag to his Mafia cronies that he extorted his Hollywood buddies out of $400,000 within six months of his arrival. Bugsy's power was evident the time he shook down Warner Brothers Studios for $10,000, warning studio execs that the guild he controlled would not provide extras for any of their films.

Bugsy's bosses saw an opportunity for Virginia to get close to Bugsy and learn as much as possible about his criminal contacts and activities, including his wire and book making operations, which the Mob eventually hoped to take over. Virginia was more than willing to be The Outfit's spy. She remembered the hot and heavy tryst that she had with Bugsy in the Big Apple a few years ago and was eager to re-establish contact with him. At a party in George Raft's house in the spring of 1939, Virginia rekindled her affair with Bugsy.

This time there would be no one night stand. The lovers spent long weekends together at Raft's house and became an item in the local media, even though Bugsy was still married and had a family in New York City. Virginia reminded people of a flamingo. Her face would flush a reddish color when she drank, just like a flamingo, and her hair had a reddish color that looked like flamingo's feathers. Bugsy began calling Virginia "The Flamingo."

Given their mercurial personalities, the affair was argumentative, tempestuous and often violent. They frequently ended up in slugfests in which Virginia got the worse of it and had to wear makeup to cover the bruises. The fighting was often over each other's lovers, but Virginia would also tear into Bugsy for not divorcing his wife. On one occasion, Bugsy nearly beat Virginia to death and then, after raping her, stormed out of her house. The incident was never reported to the police.

After the sound and the fury faded, Virginia would attempt suicide several times by over dosing on medication. Or, she and Bugsy would make up with hot and heavy sex.

WHEN NOT BRAWLING, Bugsy and Virginia worked together in joint ventures in which they ran betting scams and numbers rackets and smuggled drugs. But Bugsy's star in Mafia circles began to dim when he pled guilty to book making charges and had to pay a fine of $250. Bugsy's associates thought that Bugsy was stupid for getting nailed on such a charge and didn't like the publicity it brought the Mob. The charges were dropped, but the development made the authorities furious and more determined than ever to get Bugsy. Indeed, they began harassing Bugsy by tailing him wherever he went. Bugsy realized that he was outstaying his welcome in L.A. and made plans to leave for Las Vegas where he had lucrative gambling interests and good contacts within the law community and outside of it and could keep a low profile. Bugsy asked Virginia to go with him, but she was tired of living in a volcano and turned down the invitation.

Virginia returned to New York City where she and Joe Adonis rekindled their relationship. They were seen arm and arm around New York City and their movements were noted by local and national tabloids. Yet, still true to her nature, she continued to see other men. Virginia was truly a queenpin now, the most powerful Mob-connected woman in America.

Virginia returned once again to Los Angeles where she partied, gambled at the race track and continued to launder the Mob's money sent to her by Joe Epstein. Bugsy frequently returned to Los Angeles and literally begged Virginia to come to Las Vegas with him, but as Edmonds explained: "Virginia was loath to become involved with Las Vegas. To her it was a dirty town crawling with vulgar, sweaty men who never shaved or bathed and who treated their horses better than their women."

Virginia hated the remoteness of Las Vegas, and, besides, she was allergic to the cactus that broke her out in hives

BY THEN, BUGSY had big plans for Las Vegas where gambling was legal. In an alliance with Moe Sedway he took control of the wire services that reported the daily horse races. Sedway was a faithful lieutenant of powerful Meyer Lansky, and in the early 1930s, began making trips to Las Vegas for Lansky in order to franchise the Mob's Trans-American race wire service. By 1945 Sedway and partner Gus Greenbaum had made the El Cortez Hotel a success, turning a $4 million profit in the first year of operation alone.

One day in 1945, Bugsy took Sedway for a drive in the desert and revealed his big dream to him: "Moe, we are going to buy this hole of land and we are going to build the goddamnest biggest hotel and casino you ever saw."

Bugsy was actually on to a great idea, for Las Vegas was ready to be transformed into a tourist Mecca. Several hotels were being built or were already built—the Club Savoy, the Last Frontier, Kit Carson Club and the Golden Nugget, among others—and Bugsy's plan was not unrealistic. The way Bugsy went about building his dream, however, turned his dream project into a disaster.

Although Bugsy has been largely credited with developing Las Vegas, a man named William Wilkerson was already building a casino in the city. Wilkerson, however, was an inveterate gambler and had ran out of money. Bugsy saw a short cut to his dream and began muscling in on Wilkerson's development. To help finance his dream hotel's construction, Bugsy sold shares to his friends and associates, including Godfather Meyer Lansky who invested on behalf of the Luciano Mob. With shares selling for $250 each, Siegel was able to raise a million dollars. Bugsy hired noted designer Dell Webb with the intent of making the Flamingo the biggest hotel in Las Vegas. Siegel tried to stamp his name on his master work, naming the hotel Ben Siegel's Flamingo Hotel. The New York Mob disliked the idea of a gangster so prominently displaying his name on a venture in which it had an interest, and it sent a delegation to see Bugsy and get him to change his mind. The gangster relented and his name came off the hotel.

Bugsy was a dreamer, not a businessman, and he became so obsessed with his dream project that he recklessly poured money into the venture, sparing no expense. For example, he flew tradesmen from all over the country and paid them outrageous salaries. The hotel had to be the best and grandest, so he had the walls built double and triple thick and used only the most expensive materials.

Bugsy changed his mind often, which added thousands of dollars to the design costs. He bought building materials and had them delivered to the construction site in the morning. The delivery people who brought the materials would steal them at night and then sell them again to Bugsy the next day. The gangster was too obsessed to notice the skyrocketing bills that resulted from his workers swindling him blind out of thousands of dollars.

The costs climbed and climbed and eventually reached $6 million. The Mob was keeping an eye on its investment and looked on at developments at the Flamingo construction site with alarm. The project was out of control, and the Mob realized it would be an impossible task to recoup its investment.

VIRGINIA CONTINUED TO stay away from Vegas. Bugsy, despite the pressure of the Flamingo Project, returned to L.A. often, and, despite their quarrels, the lovers continued to spend long weekends together in bed. In their pillow talk, the topic of the Flamingo hotel came up. Virginia learned that Bugsy was not only losing a fortune he was skimming thousands of dollars from the project. Bugsy confided to Virginia, that when something needed to be done, he over charged the project to the Nevada Projects Corporation, which he had formed to oversee the project. If, for instance, the actual cost was $20,000, he would charge the corporation $40,000 and pocket the difference. She kept track of the money in her diary, and when she added the figures up, the skimming came to nearly $2 million.

The New York mobsters were no fools. Luciano and his associates knew all the corruption tricks and they picked up on what was going on.

Bugsy was now in deep trouble with the Mob. Compounding his problems was the fact that he was also running out of money. He knew he had to open the hotel pronto to save the venture. Desperate and realizing his life was at stake, Bugsy called on Billy Wilkerson and asked him to help pay off the debt in return for a bigger share of the hotel. Bugsy also asked Wilkerson if he could ask his Hollywood pals to come to the opening of the Flamingo so that the event would attract big media coverage. And, oh yes, Siegel confided to Wilkerson, that it is important my Mob friends in New York not find out about your investment. Mums the word, Wilkerson assured Bugsy.

ON DECEMBER 26, 1946, the Flamingo opened, but only the casino, restaurant and showroom were ready. The New York Mob wanted Bugsy to wait until the hotel itself was ready, but he went ahead anyway and opened. The opening was to be a gala occasion attracting much good publicity, but a number of the Hollywood celebs—Clark Gable, Spencer Tracy, William Holden and Lucille Ball, among others—said they had previous engagements and did not attend. Bugsy spent nearly $22,000 on newspaper ads, but most of them appeared only in the local media.

With the big night approaching, Virginia decided to go to Vegas. It was not a good move. The pressure mounted and Bugsy would explode, scream and slug Virginia. By now, the Mob Queen was an emotional wreck. She wanted to leave, but Bugsy asked her to wait until at least through the Flamingo's opening month.

If Bugsy did not already have enough problems, Mother Nature stepped in and gave a kick to the gangster's declining fortunes by deluging Vegas with rain. Opening night was a total washout. To save the opening, Bugsy staged a special "Hollywood Weekend," a few days after Christmas. Partner Wilkerson persuaded some of Hollywood's stars to show up, but "Hollywood Weekend" was another disaster and Bugsy lost a half million dollars.

Virginia left for L.A. where she was literally a basket case and very difficult to be with. Prone to fits of violent temper, she even threatened to kill some guests at a private party at her L.A. home on North Linden Drive.

Nothing could save Bugsy's Flamingo project, and he closed the casino on February 1, 1947. Ironically, the Flamingo re-opened in March 1947, as Las Vegas was about to take off as a tourist Mecca, and this time the Flamingo began making money. The Luciano Mob, however, was finished with Bugsy. At a meeting held in late May, 1947, the Mob decided that Bugsy would have to go. The question was whether Virginia Hill would be taken out with Bugsy.

Many in the Mob felt that Virginia had outlived her usefulness, and during her long affair with Bugsy changed for the worse. Other Mob members could care less about whether Virginia lived or died. After the Mob made its decision, Virginia got a call on June 8, ordering her to pack her bags and leave town. Eight days later, Virginia met Joe Epstein at Chicago's Midway Airport. Epstein gave Virginia $5,000 and she boarded a plane for Paris, France, knowing full well what was going to happen to Bugsy. Soon, he would be out of her life forever.

ON JUNE 20, Bugsy finished his business and went to Virginia's Beverly Hills mansion to relax with some friends. After the friends left, Bugsy sat down in the living room to read the newspaper. The drapes were open, giving the killer with a gun a clear view of Bugsy. Nine shots rang out in rapid fire. When the shooting stopped, three of Bugsy's friends ran into the living room and saw Bugsy slumped on the sofa, blood streaming from his head and gushing from the socket of one of his eyes. Benjamin Bugsy Siegel was buried in a $5,000 silver-plated casket but only five people attended his funeral. The Los Angles police never did solve the murder.

The police questioned Virginia about Bugsy's death, but she claimed she was never really friendly with Bugsy.

"I never knew Ben was involved in all that gang stuff," Virginia said. "He never mentioned anything about it, and I never asked him questions. I never saw him before he got started on the Flamingo."

AFTER BUGSY'S MURDER, Virginia's life continued to unravel. She got chronically depressed and became a loud, nasty drunk in public gatherings. She would drink herself into oblivion and tried to commit suicide several times. To get away from her problems, she traveled in Latin America and finally settled in Mexico City where, given the notoriety, she could not help but be the center of attention.

Virginia struggled to get her life straight, and it looked as if it took a turn for the better in February 1950 when she met Norman Johann "Hans" Hauser, a dashing and handsome Austrian ski instructor who was working at a ski resort in Sun Valley. Virginia married Hauser within months of their meeting and they had a son.

Hauser, however, was a non U.S. citizen and he ran into immigration problems because he was suspected of being a Nazi sympathizer during World War II. Virginia generated a stream of publicity trying to free her husband from the clutches of the U.S. Immigration and Naturalization Service. When none of the former Mob Queen's friends or associates stepped forward to help with her husband's predicament, she began blabbing to the press about her Mob connections, her money laundering activities for the Mob and the secret diary she had kept, which the press dubbed "Virginia Hill's most excellent life insurance plan."

The move backfired when Virginia's comments caught the attention of a new U.S. Senate Committee formed to investigate crime in the U.S. Chaired by Estes Kefauver, a tall and broad shouldered but courtly senator from Tennessee. The investigation, popularly known as the Kefauver Hearings, were held live on television from May 30, 1950, to May 3, 1951. At a time, when many Americans were buying their first television set, and fascinated by the new medium, millions stayed glued to their TV screens. Estes Kefauver became famous, as a result of the Committee exposure, and went on to make a run for the American presidency. The Committee brought to public attention formerly obscure gangsters like Meyer Lansky, Frank Costello, Joe Adonis and Lucky Luciano.

Virginia was subpoenaed to appear before the Committee, which thought she could provide information about Chicago's book making operations. She was scheduled to appear before the Committee in Chicago on September 29, 1950, but got a delay because she was pregnant.

When Virginia finally appeared before the Kefauver Committee in March 1950, her performance was mesmerizing and explosive, her language salty. She called the mob of reporters greeting her every day a bunch of "cheap fucking bastards" and attempted to portray herself as fun loving party girl and not a

Mob Queen. She yelled at committee members and pounded her fist on the table when asked questions she did not like. And her answer to every question was vague and evasive. When she had finished her testimony, Virginia thought she had gotten the best of the Committee, but Uncle Sam had a trump card to play. The IRS indicted her for tax fraud and served her with a lien of $161,000 for back income taxes for the years 1942 through 1947.

Virginia lost the case and nearly everything she owned, including her beautiful Los Angeles home and her wedding ring. Fed up with the U.S. government, a bitter Virginia Hill applied for and received an Austrian passport on September 25, 1951. Once safely out of the country, Virginia publicly blasted the politicians in Washington, calling them "rats" and vowing never to return to America. Uncle Sam, though, was not through with Virginia. The Treasury Department issued a Virginia Hill Wanted Poster, the first time the U.S. government had issued a Wanted Poster against a woman for tax evasion.

Eventually Hill tried to work out a deal with Uncle Sam that would allow her to return to the U.S., but considered the attached strings outrageous and totally unacceptable. Broke and desperate, Virginia drew on her insurance policy—the secret diary. Uncle Sam was interested but it could not reach an agreement with Virginia and a deal fell through.

VIRGINIA NOW DECIDED to throw caution to the wind and contacted Joe Epstein and Joe Adonis, her two old Mob contacts. In effect, she blackmailed them, threatening that she would reveal the contents of her diary unless they gave her a "settlement." Joe Adonis sent Virginia $3,000 in cash, but the former Mob Queen sent him a letter, decrying the paltry sum of money and warning she that she could get more for the diary if she sold it on the open market. Adonis sent Virginia another $3000, but Virginia still demanded more money. At a meeting with Adonis in Naples, Virginia upped her demand to $10,000.

ON MARCH 24, 1966, hikers found the body of 49-year old Virginia Hill near a brook in Koppl, Austria, a small town near Salzburg. Virginia's death was ruled a suicide, but it is still widely believed that the Mob had her murdered because she knew too much and could not be reasoned with. Today, her diary is reportedly in the hands of a Chicago underworld figure.

Nearly a half century later, Virginia Hill is a legendary Mob Queen by any standard. No woman before or since her, has risen as high as she did in the ranks of the La Cosa Nostra.

SIX

The Queen of the DC Underworld

IF **WASHINGTON DC** has a gangster, dead or alive, who can measure up to Chicago's Al Capone or New York City's John Gotti and the legendary gangsters from other major cities, Odessa Madre would be a prime candidate. Her name may not resonate with today's younger gang bangers, but there are still a few old-timers who remember the woman who became known as the Queen of the DC Underworld.

Odessa got that moniker because she dominated the DC's criminal underworld for nearly half a century. She was into nearly everything illicit—gambling, prostitution, numbers and graft. One police affidavit filed in U.S. District Court in 1975 said: "Odessa practices a resourceful and shrewd form of circumspection that has enabled her to survive and thrive in illegal activities over the past 40 years."

In 1990, Miller A. Dixon, a retired DC police department sergeant, who, at the time was 77-years old, said this of the Queen of the Underworld: "I had a lot of respect for Odessa. She was the only person I ever met who had just made the decision early on life to be bad. She said: 'to hell with it and went on about her business.'"

Odessa Madre

Being bad meant Odessa was always in trouble with the law. The cops picked her up at least 30 times on 57 charges, as her narcotics and prostitution activities made her familiar figure to law enforcement.

Yet, despite her legal problems, Odessa did not keep a low profile. For instance, she was known to give big parties at her home where she regularly put out bowls of heroin, cocaine and marijuana for her guests. With a twinkle in her eye, she would insist that the stories about her largesse were not exactly true.

"Everybody knows I can't stand them reefers (marijuana cigarettes)," she once told the *Washington Post*.

Unlike many queenpins, Odessa Madre did not grow up poor. Born the only child of a seamstress and a baker, Odessa inherited property that made her economically better off than most of the black brothers and sisters living in DC during the time. From the sketchy accounts of Odessa's life, it appears that her parents spoiled her rotten. Because of her sewing skill,

Odessa's mother dressed up her daughter in fine clothes, while her father let the child empty the till of his business without reprimanding her.

Odessa's ancestors were a part of the black migration that had trekked to the DC region as indentured servants and slaves. Later, an area of the city was named Madre Park after her grandfather, a civil war veteran. The local slaves were emancipated on April 16, 1862, nine months before President Abraham Lincoln made his famous Emancipation Proclamation. Yet, despite the ensuing racism, DC African Americans managed to build a vibrant community. Between 1920 and 1930, Washington's black population jumped 20 percent.

The Washington.org web site noted: "By seeking out opportunity and succeeding in education, businesses and the arts, DC's black population became integral in the development of Washington DC."

In Odessa Madre's formative years, DC had strict segregationist policies in place and that extended all the way to the White House. For example, President Woodrow Wilson, who actually considered himself to be a progressive, refused to hire blacks as federal employees and had no qualms about segregating federal offices. It was not until 1961 that President Kennedy appointed a black commissioner.

There were a lot of Irish people living in Odessa's neighborhood, and because they allowed the cows to roam the alleys freely, the area became known as Cow Town. The Irish and the African Americans got along, which was a good thing for Odessa later in life because many of the Irish from Cow Town became cops. Odessa was able to cultivate relationships with the Irish cops when she became a notorious underworld queen.

Later, Odessa recalled: "Negroes and Irishmen got along real well. They would fight among themselves. If somebody outside of Cow Town came to fight the Irish, the Negroes would chuck bricks at them. We were like a big happy family."

ODESSA ATTENDED DUNBAR High School, an educational institution to which prominent black families from around the country sent their children. Dunbar High School is located in the Truxton Circle neighborhood of Northwest Washington, and today it serves grades 9 to 12 as part of the District of Colombia public school system. As DC's first high school for black students, the school was eventually named in honor of noted poet Paul Lawrence Dunbar. Its illustrious faculty included Carter G. Woodson, a historian, author and journalist; Anna Julie Cooper, an author, educator and scholar; and Mary Church Terrell, one of the first African Americans to earn a college degree. Graduates included Sterling Brown, an African American professor; Charles R. Drew, an African American surgeon, physician and medical researcher; and Charles Hamilton Houston, an African American lawyer and dean of the Howard Law School. Dunbar High was the type of educational institution from which its students would head up the professional career ladder as far as Jim Crow racism would allow.

Odessa showed promise of being one of Dunbar's illustrious graduates. Her aunt had graduated from M Street High School, the forerunner of Dunbar, and helped get Odessa into the elite school. The aunt lived in LeDroit Park, a middle class black neighborhood populated largely by academics, and she and her preacher husband provided Odessa with a tutor in mathematics and oratory.

While all the students at Dunbar were African American, the shades of pigmentation among the students allowed racism to permeate the school's environment.

In 1980, Odessa told the *Washington Post*, "They'd call me the big black mutha… There were only three blacks at Dunbar back then—I mean black like me. I had good diction, I knew the gestures but they always made fun of me."

Odessa provided the *Washington Post* reporter with a graphic example, "On those days when we are having drill competition and we were suppose to wear the school colors, I would say: 'Oh, big black Dessa—you don't have to wear the school colors, just stick out your big fat red tongue.'"

Despite the bad experience at Dunbar, Odessa did well and graduated with honors. Her next move, at the time typical for a Dunbar graduate, would have been to enroll at DC's Howard University. But she was turned off to the idea of further schooling because she expected to face the same kind of harassment she experienced at Dunbar.

SO EVEN WITH the ripe opportunities presented to her, Odessa had other plans. She was still a teenager but her ambitions made her swear off men. In fact, she liked to call herself "The Black Widow." Odessa decided that she would make a lot of money in life and she was not going to be particular in how she did it. She started slowly in her life of crime but would eventually build an empire of numbers banks, whore houses and drinking establishments.

Odessa received an inheritance from the money her family made selling Madre Park, and she used it to buy two houses in her old neighborhood. Odessa kept one for herself and used the other one to sell bootleg liquor.

With no real competition, Odessa became a major boot-legger. But not content to rest on her laurels, Odessa quickly expanded into gambling and prostitution. By the mid 1940s, she had a large bookmaking operation and six bawdy houses that employed 20 women. Odessa's entrepreneurial ways, both legal and illegal, helped make her a very rich woman. The *Washington Post* reported that at the height of her success she was making $100,000 annually.

EVEN THOUGH ODESSA was just starting out as a criminal, it is understandable why bootleggers and other gangsters were willing to do business with her. They thought she would protect them from the law, especially after rumors began circulating that Odessa was in good with the police. Indeed, knowing Odessa could pay dividends if you were a policeman wanting to move up the DC police department's bureaucratic hierarchy.

Miller Dixon was country boy from Honea Path, South Carolina, who moved to DC and became a cop in the early 1940s. As a young rookie patrolman assigned to the sanitation department, Dixon noticed that Odessa owned a dog, and so he went to her house to see if she had a dog license. Odessa had no fear of the police, and she let the young patrolman in. To Dixon's amazement, he discovered a bustling after-hour's night spot in Odessa's basement. Welcome to the DC underworld.

Dixon may have been green to the police force, but he was wise enough not to arrest Odessa. Instead, he used her to gather information about the DC underworld, a move that no doubt helped Dixon rise through the ranks of the DC police force to the position of detective.

"Odessa knew all about how prostitutes operated and about how things are done outside the law in general," Dixon recalled at the time of Odessa's death. "She was very knowledgeable about con games and she knew all the tricks of the pro-shoplifters' trade."

Odessa's headquarters at 2204 14 St. NW became known as Club Madre, a well known night spot that was frequented by many black celebrities. One of the most famous was Duke Ellington, a prominent jazz figure and a DC native. Ellington was born in 1899 to James and Dorothy Ellington, but he lived with his maternal grandparents in the West End neighborhood of DC. Ellington was known for jazz but he delved in all types of music, from blues to gospel to classical. Ellington left a promising musical career in DC but returned often to the city, where he would perform frequently at Club Madre.

Boxers Joe Louis and singer Nat King Cole were two of the legendary celebrities who could be seen at Club Madre on certain nights. Odessa became close to standup comedian Jackie "Moms" Mobley who reportedly played for free at the club. Mobley was a prominent performer in the so-called Circuit of African American Vaudeville, earning as much as $10,000 a week at Harlem's Apollo Theater. In the summer of 1969, Mobley became the oldest person ever to have a Top 40 Hit on the billboard charts where her satirical version of the song "Abraham, Martin and John" hit number 35.

Odessa was known to make theatrical entrances to her club at the appropriate moment when the Who's Who of Black DC were all seated. In a September 28, 1980, *Washington Post* profile of Odessa, Courtland Malloy wrote: "Odessa would make her grand entrance into the club, mink from ear to ankle. That was a lot of mink, because she weighed about 260 pounds back then. Reserved, in the center of the room, was a table vacant except for a dozen, long-stemmed roses. Odessa would lead an entourage—a trail of about six or seven beautiful 'yella girls,' mostly all for sale, followed by a train of lusty, well heeled E-lite gents."

Odessa also owned the Flamingo Lounge at 2204 14th Street NW, where more famous celebrities, such as jazz great Charley Parker, appeared, and pop singer Lloyd Price's backup musicians made up the house band. The Flamingo was so popular that people had to come to the club early; otherwise, they could not get in. Odessa sold the club to Walker Bernard Johnson in 1957, but after a decade, the club declined in popularity and closed.

DURING WORLD WAR II, Odessa and another noted DC gangster named Roger "Whitetop" Simkins started a numbers bank at 1719 1ˢᵗ Street NW, which became known as "The Night Number." Simkins was a popular gambling king who got his nickname "Whitetop" because his hair had begun turning prematurely white. He became a numbers banker in 1940, beginning with a small bank with two employees and using a restaurant called the Owl Lunchroom as a front.

By 1945 he was a major figure in the DC numbers racket, reportedly grossing up to $8,000 a day. Simkins was arrested several times but only spent a short time in prison around 1964.

A 1952 report of a congressional committee, which was investigating crime and law enforcement in the District, noted that: "There is much evidence that his relations with the Metropolitan Police Force were extensive and intimate."

The report revealed that police officers regularly visited his numbers headquarters to pay for protection.

In February 1952, Simkins refused to reveal whether he gave former police chief Robert J. Barrett "gifts," worth more than $500, on the grounds that presenting such information would incriminate him.

The congressional committee noted that from July 1, 1947, when Barrett became DC's Superintendent of Police: "Simkins size and power as a racketeer increased with ever increasing responsibility."

The committee further reported that Simkins expanded his operation, adding several more numbers banks, but none were ever "molested" by police. In fact, Simkins began to crowd other numbers bankers out of the field. At times, Simkins congressional committee testimony bordered on the bizarre.

Arnold Bauman (committee counsel): What is your business or occupation?

Simkins: I refuse to answer on the grounds that it may tend to incriminate me.

Bauman: Your name is Roger Simkins?

Simkins: That's correct.

Mr. Bauman: S-I-M-K-I-N-S.

Simkins: That is correct.

Bauman: Your first name is spelled R-O-G-E-R?

Simkins: That is correct.

Bauman: Have you described yourself as a speculator?

Simkins: I refuse to answer on the grounds it may incriminate me.

Bauman: You are also known as Whitetop. Is that correct?

Simkins: I refuse to answer on the grounds it may incriminate me.

Senator Herman Weller (of Idaho): I hope and the committee hopes that by inadvertence you are not letting the witness get into trouble by a silly answer such as that. We don't want our action here to mislead you to the point where he might be found in contempt. Now a man's name would certainly not tend to incriminate him.

Simkins' counsel was then advised that, by not answering, their client would be subjected to further hearings and legal expenses. Simkins then relented and acknowledged his nickname was Whitetop, but offered little else.

ODESSA CAME UNDER intense public scrutiny, too, when the Kefauver Committee asked her to testify before it. Estes Kefauver, the committee's chairman, a tall-broad-shouldered and charismatic senator from Tennessee, held hearings live on television from May 1950 to May 1951. At that time, when many Americans were buying their first television set, Kefauver became famous as a result of the committee's exposure. He later made a failed run for the American presidency.

Testimony before the Kefauver Committee revealed that Odessa Madre was a major organized crime figure who was protected by the Washington DC police force through payoffs. Two sergeants in the force testified that they had been demoted and re-assigned to school-crossing duty because they had assisted in the arrest of Odessa and other gamblers and had refused a payoff from Odessa. Other policemen testified that Odessa had paid police superintendent James Barrett $2,000 a month in so-called "ice" payments.

Nearly three decades later, Odessa defended her actions, arguing: "Somebody had to give them money. If anybody was lucky enough to get protection, it was because they were lucky enough to have my recommendation to the police. That's how it worked. I would tell the police if you were okay and if it was going to be worth their while. Then you give me the money and I would make the drop. They wouldn't take it from anybody."

In 1952 Odessa had no qualms about providing authorities with information about the numbers racket in DC. She described how the "ice," the slang word used for police protection in DC, was an integral part of the cost of doing business, which amounted to a $5,000 to $7,000 daily take. Madre revealed that the local numbers racket was being supervised by a Whitetop underling while Whitetop was in Arkansas getting a divorce. So it was a good time to undercut Whitetop. But Odessa's motivation? She wanted revenge because she found Simkins was getting ready to double cross her and go into business with another racketeer named Pullin' Head Jones.

Odessa Madre with her lawyer in 1952

Odessa was as good at spending money as she was at making it, and her lavish ways made newspaper headlines. She blew money on expensive clothes and trips, and was known to buy exotic cars, especially after being released from prison. For instance, in 1968 she bought a Lincoln Continental with a vanity "Madre" license plate. In 1980, it was a Cadillac Seville.

The DC-based *Afro American* magazine reported how she once entered a store reserved for whites, fully expecting the white store clerk to wait on her. Instead, the store clerk summoned her manager. When Odessa began pulling out rolls of hundred dollar bills, the store clerk fainted. Madre then commanded the store manager to bring her the finest fur coat in the store. He readily complied. In fact, he brought two fur coats.

Odessa surveyed the fur coats with a haughty look and proclaimed: "This is nothing but crap." Then with an imperious manner, she returned to her chauffeured limousine.

Odessa was known to have a generous heart, and she gave away a lot of money to friend and stranger a like. She would befriend somebody in the street and give them money, and she would give the children in her neighborhood money just for being good kids. She would even help pay for funerals.

Not all of Washington, though, was enamored with the life, spirit and exploits of Odessa Madre. When the *Washington Post* ran a profile of Odessa in its September 28, 1980, magazine issue, the newspaper received some critical letters, which it printed. C.B. Boskin of Severna Park, Maryland, wrote: "I'm absolutely astounded at your colossal bad taste in having that dreadful woman on the cover of the magazine. Who wants to read about the queen of the Washington underworld?"

Shimon D. Magen, who identified himself as being from DC, was equally critical, noting that Odessa was not a philanthropist, statesman or businessman but a "septuagenarian ex-madam and former boss of gambling rackets." He complained that the *Post* quoted the "Lady as saying, 'crime does pay.'"

UNFORTUNATELY FOR ODESSA, her high profile appearance before the Kefauver Committee meant that she would be constantly in trouble with the law for the rest of her life, although the fact is she had a steady string of arrests dating back to 1935. In July 1945 she was convicted of a gambling charge and paid a $150 fine.

In 1958 Odessa got out of jail after serving more than 13 years for a robbery conviction. Then she was caught in a police dragnet involving 17 raids on suspected gambling locations around DC. In arresting Odessa at her home, Inspector Robert L. Dillard described her as head of one of the city's largest numbers rings, estimating that her ring did an annual business of at least $3 million.

That same year, the authorities went to Odessa's home to serve her a grand jury subpoena. Odessa tried to convince the authorities she was too ill to appear in court by opening a dresser door and showing them her medicine. But the police saw a handgun and arrested her. Two years later, Odessa was convicted of operating a numbers bank and was sentenced to serve from three to seven years in prison.

In 1961 Odessa was jailed pending a hearing regarding a year-old conviction for receiving stolen property. Twelve days later, her bond was revoked when she was charged in an unrelated narcotics case. She faced five years in jail, if convicted. Police seized the 17 capsules of heroin when they raided her home. Odessa pleaded guilty to possessing an amount worth about $1,500 on the illicit market Odessa managed to stay free on appeal until 1977 when the U.S. Court of Appeals reduced her sentence to three years.

The constant legal battles broke Odessa financially, and she was nearly destitute when she got out of jail. It did not help either that her house sitter wrote $15,000 in bad checks while she was locked up. Odessa needed a job badly, so friends helped her get one as a counselor with the United Planning Organization. By then, however, she was a senior citizen and so found the job too tiring. The financial stress took its toll and her weight dropped from more than 200 pounds to about 110 pounds. Still, Odessa managed to wax philosophical about her situation.

"Into each life a little rain must fall," she said. "I'm thankful for having made it thus far. The good times are gone but not forgotten."

IN SEPTEMBER 1995, the *National Catholic Reporter* magazine published a fascinating article that chronicled Odessa's relationship with an ex-Catholic priest and missionary named

Hubert Sonnenschein. In a flattering portrait, the magazine described Odessa as: "Succeeding in her world as well as Hubert had in missionary work and as being generous as well as she was colorful…"

Both Odessa and Hubert were on kidney dialysis when they met at a dialysis center iñ DC in 1987. They would sit next to each other in rocking chairs in a room that had 40 other dialysis patients. The *National Catholic Reporter* described their relationship as: "Being as close as Jesus and the woman at the well."

While they rocked and talked, Hubert noticed that Odessa was starving and how at times she became delusional. Hubert could see that nobody was feeding Odessa. Under Hubert's guidance, however, the situation changed. When it was time to leave the dialysis center, he organized the other patients to help Odessa and ensure that she was better taken care of.

THREE MONTHS LATER, in February 1990, Odessa Madre, a woman who at one time had been one of the richest people in DC, died penniless at age 83. It took eight days for family members to claim her body. Her friends were able to raise $51 for her funeral, but W.H. Bacon of the Bacon Funeral Home stepped forward to ensure she would not be buried in a cheap casket.

"She helped a lot of people," Bacon told the press. "She deserved better. She gave me money to bury friends throughout the years."

Not everybody was impressed with Odessa Madre. In a letter to the editor of the *Washington Post*, Patrick Goggins described Odessa as a remorseless criminal who was arrested 37 times.

"In a city in which crime is a critical problem, let us not exult criminals. Why not instead hold up as models the hundreds of police officers who risk their lives every day in an effort to stop the District's biggest problem?"

Still, whatever one might think about Odessa's legacy, she was an original gangster and, no doubt, the Queen of the DC Underworld.

SEVEN

Radical Icon: Gangster or Revolutionary Queenpin?

T HE LATE 1960S and early 1970s was a time of fervent Black Nationalism in America when many young African American became radicalized by the traumatic events sweeping the country. The Vietnam War raged and its ending was nowhere in sight. In 1964 President Lyndon Baines Johnson declared "War on Poverty" and promised America a "Great Society." Change did come, but its pace frustrated many young blacks. The civil rights movement had gained strength and the U.S. Congress passed many laws to end discrimination and segregation. Yet, many young blacks believed America was an inherently racist society incapable of transforming itself into a just one.

Radicalized young blacks joined the Black Panther Party, which championed itself as "Defenders of America's Black People." Founded in1966 in Oakland, California by Bobby Seale and Huey Newton, the party's ten point program called for "Land, Bread, Housing, Education, Justice and Peace," as well as for the exemption of blacks from military service. The party quickly expanded into many U.S., cities and its membership reached 5,000.

One of the young blacks who joined the Black Panther Party in 1970 was 23-year old Joanne Deborah Byron, who would later change her name to Assata Shakur. In Shakur's words, "I decided that the most important thing in my life was for me to struggle for the liberation of black people."

But Shakur quit the Party not long after because it was not radical enough for her and joined an even more radical organization, the Black Liberation Army. From 1971 to 1973, Shakur believed in and called for revolution in the U.S.. She was also suspected of being involved in a series of bank robberies and attacks on police in New York, New Jersey, Detroit and St. Louis.

In her war upon the American status quo, Shakur's life took a dramatic turn on May 2, 1973, about 12:45 a.m., when the two-door Pontiac Lemans she was in was stopped by police on the New Jersey Turnpike. The events that followed have made her, on one hand, a pariah of the American establishment and one of U.S. law enforcement's most wanted criminals, and, on the other, a legendary icon for the country's radical left.

NEW JERSEY STATE trooper James Harper stopped the Pontiac Lemans with the Vermont license plates because, he later reported, it had a broken tail light and was "slightly" exceeding the speed limit on the turnpike. In the car with Shakur, who sat in the right front seat, was the driver, Zayd Malik Shakur (born James F. Costan), and Sundiata Acoli (born Clark Squire) who sat in the right rear seat.

Trooper Werner Foerster pulled up in a second patrol car to act as a backup to Harper who reported on the police dispatch that he had stopped the car. In a dispatch recording played later at the trial of Assata Shakur and Sundiata Acoli, Harper could be heard saying: "Hold on—two black males and one female."

Trooper Harper asked Zayd Shakur for some identification but noticed a discrepancy in what he was shown. So Harper asked Shakur to step out of the car and follow him to the rear. At this point, the testimony presented by the prosecution and the defense later at the trial differ.

Harper testified that Foerster reached into the vehicle and pulled out and held up an automatic pistol and ammunition clip, exclaiming: "Jim look what I found."

Both Assata Shakur and Acoli were ordered to put their hands on their laps and not to move. Harper testified that Assata Shakur reached down to the right of her right leg, pulled out a pistol and shot Harper in the right shoulder, after which Harper managed to move behind his vehicle. Then according to Harper, Assata Shakur used the wounded Foerster's own gun to execute him. Harper testified that he shot and wounded Assata as she killed Foerster. The wounded Assata, along with Acoli and the dying Zayd Shakur, fled in the Pontiac Lemans with three patrol cars in hot pursuit. The car finally stopped five miles down the road across from the Joyce Kilmer Service Area.

Acoli jumped out of the car and fled into the woods, as officers shouted for him to stop and emptied their guns. According to the testimony of one officer at the scene, Assata walked toward him with her bloody arm waving surrender. After a 36-hour manhunt involving 400 police officers and other people, Acoli was captured. Meanwhile, police found Zayd Shakur's body along the road in a nearby gulley.

Trooper Harper survived the wound in his left shoulder and remained in good condition under protective guard at the hospital. Assata Shakur was arraigned from her hospital bed while receiving medical care. The State of New Jersey could hardly wait to get Assata Shakur, the revolutionary whom they said was a cop-killer, on trial.

IT WAS A remarkable turning point in the life of a young black woman who did not seem destined for notoriety as one of the U.S. most famous revolutionaries accused of involvement in gangster activities. Assata Shakur was born in New York City on July 16, 1947. Her parents divorced when she was three years old, and she went to live with her aunt and grandparents, Frank and Lulu Hill, in Jamaica, New York. Shakur accompanied her grandparents to Wilmington North Carolina, where she spent her early childhood.

It was the segregated south and Shakur was barred from the public beaches. Shakur recalled later how much she wanted to go to a beautiful park and zoo she and her grandparents had passed one day. The young girl would "beg whine and nay" her grandmother to take her to the zoo, and when she did not, Shakur thought her grandmother to be the world's meanest woman. Then one day her grandmother explained to Shakur that they were not allowed into the zoo because they were black.

Shakur's grandparents were big on respect, with one precondition, Shakur recalled in her autobiography: "I was taught to be polite and respectful to adults, to say good morning and good evening as I passed the neighbor's house. Any kind of back talk or sass was simply out of the question. But the grandparents expected it to be reciprocated and they would drill into the young girl: 'Don't let anybody disrespect you… Hear me? We're not raising you up to be mistreated, you hear? I don't want you taking sass from nobody, you understand?'"

Her grandparent valued education and instilled in their grandchild a love of the written word. Shakur spent a lot time reading books her grandparents brought from the "colored library." Realizing the young girl would get an inferior education in the South, the grandparents sent Shakur south to live with her mother and stepfather in New York City. Suddenly, she was thrust into a new environment that was the polar opposite to the all-black segregated one she had left. Her new neighborhood was nearly all-white,

Assata Shakur

middle class and heavily Jewish. Now she was the only black kid in class, and as she grew older, Shakur began noticing the big difference between black and white, rich and poor.

Shakur's education continued, thanks in large part to her aunt Evelyn, whom she describes as the heroine of her childhood. Aunt Evelyn would take her to museums, plays, movies and to all kinds of restaurants.

In high school, Shakur began questioning everything around her. The youngster would be days late getting home and was always, it seemed, in trouble. She began running away from home, too. Her life on the streets was hard, but it was an education. Shakur worked at odd jobs, befriended a transvestite, stayed with a family of professional shoplifters and found herself in some dangerous situations before her aunt Evelyn found and took her home. Shakur quit high school for good at age 16, but Aunt Evelyn saw to it that Shakur earned her Graduate Equivalent Degree (GED).

Remarkably, in the late 1960s, Shakur still managed to enroll in Manhattan Community College, intent on majoring in business and getting a job in marketing or advertising when she graduated. But she was drawn to the college's growing black studies program and to student activism. As Shakur noted, black consciousness and nationalism were on the upswing. Shakur began reading everything she could find about black history, culture and ideology, joined black student groups and engaged in heated debates and exchanges about racial matters at meetings. She changed her hair, wore African looking dresses and became a committed activist.

"It was like being born again," Shakur wrote. "It was then that I decided that the most important thing in my life was for me to struggle for the liberation of black people."

Shakur married Louis Chesimard, but eventually changed her name to Assata Shakur. As she explained the name change: "I decided on Assata Olugbala Shakur: 'He who struggles.' Olugbula means 'Love for people,' and I took the name Shakur out of respect for Zayd and Zayd's family. Shakur means: 'The thankful.'"

THE MAKING OF the black revolutionary was complete when she joined the Black Panther Party. Growing up, Shakur never thought about being a revolutionary, but that was all she could think of now.

Shakur later recalled: "As much as I dug the Party, I always had some differences with its style of work."

Shakur concluded that the Black Party was weak and ineffectual and lacked a unifying philosophy. So she turned to an even more radical black organization, the Black Liberation Army (BLA), which believed in armed struggle and violence to bring about revolutionary change. The BLA was a black nationalist

Marxist radical organization that operated from 1970 to 1981 and was composed largely of former disaffected Black Panther members.

According to a U.S. Justice Department report on BLA activities, the organization was suspected of involvement in more than 60 incidents of violence between 1960 and 1976. The Fraternal Order of Police blamed the BLA for the murder of 13 police officers.

One New York detective, John Flynn, told the *Philadelphia Inquirer*: "The BLA figured that, in fomenting violence against the political establishment, the police would overreact and attack the black community. When that happened, they believed they would be able to enlist other blacks in their fight."

On August 29, 1972, the BLA claimed responsibility for the murder of 51-year old John Victor Young, a San Francisco police officer who was shot dead while working at his desk in a police station. Two months later, Officer James R. Greene, an Atlanta police officer was shot and killed in his patrol van at a gas station. Two BLA members were identified as being responsible for the killing. Shakur would be personally charged with six different crimes, including bank robbery and the attempted murder of police officers.

On April 6, 1971, Shakur was shot in the stomach during an altercation with a guest at the Statler Hilton Hotel in Midtown Manhattan. After an August 23, 1971, bank robbery, Shakur was sought for questioning and became one of four people suspected by New York City police of a hand grenade attack that destroyed a police car and slightly injured two patrolmen in Queens, New York City. Shakur became the subject of a nationwide manhunt in 1972 when the FBI identified her as a BLA cell leader who was involved in a serious of cold blooded murders of New York City police officers. By this time, Shakur was also being identified as a radical black leader.

A photo allegedly taken of Shakur at the bank robbery appeared as a full page advertisement on July 10, 1972, in the New York Daily News, announcing that Shakur was wanted for robbery and offering a $20,000 reward for information leading to her capture. A duplicate of the photo was placed in every bank in the city and State of New York, as well as post offices and subway stations.

Later Shakur claimed she was shocked by the news of killings of police men, but added, "Somebody was finally doing what the rest of us only had fantasies about."

Since her escape from prison, Shakur has revealed little about her involvement in BLA activities. As Margo V. Perkins wrote in her book, *Autobiography as Activism*, "Her narrative is largely concerned with defending herself against bogus changes for crimes she didn't commit. Whether there were crimes she did commit in the course of her activist work remains notably vague."

SHAKUR IS ONE of several American radicals claiming to be targeted by the FBI's COINTELPRO, an acronym for Counter Intelligence Program. COINTELPRO, which begun in 1956 and was terminated in 1971, was an overt un-American attempt by the U.S. government to stifle political dissent. The FBI's justification for COINTELPRO was that the program would "neutralize civil rights, anti-war and other programs that were nothing more than communist front organizations."

As J. Edgar Hoover, the former FBI Director, explained, "The forces that are most anxious to undermine our internal security are not things easy to identify. Communists have been trained in deceit and secretly want to work toward the day when they hope to supplant our American way of life. While they, as individuals, are difficult to identify, the Communist Party line is clear. Its first concern is the advent of the Soviet Russia and the godless communist cause. It is important to know the enemies of the American way of life."

The FBI conducted more than 2000 COINTELPRO operations before the program was publicly exposed in 1971 after a large number of documents were stolen from the FBI office in the town of Media, Pennsylvania. More documents came to light when several people who believed they were being targeted by COINTELPRO sued the U.S. government. The documents revealed that the FBI used a number of disruptive techniques, including burglaries, the illegal opening and photocopying of first-class mail, anonymous letters containing false statements designed to foment violence against the Black Panthers, anonymous letters to spouses designed to break up marriages, and the planting of documents to make it appear individuals were government informants. The FBI used COINTELPRO to target five groups that were perceived as threats to national security. They included the Communist Party, the Socialist Workers Party, white hate gangs, Black Nationalist 'hate' groups and New Left organizations.

COINTELPRO's "Black Nationalist Program" targeted a range of organizations from the radical Black Panther Party to the moderate Southern Christian Leadership Conference. According to a report by the *West Encyclopedia of American Law*, "In order to eliminate the Black Nationalist groups (that) are considered dangerous, the FBI conspired with police departments to target specific individuals, name them of crimes they did not commit, suppress exculpatory evidence and falsely incarcerate them."

The exposure of COINTELPRO and its dirty tactics led to a public outcry and an investigation by U.S. Congress. The House report was kept secret; the Senate's report was not, and it was released on April 28, 1976, by the so called Church Committee that Idaho Senator Frank Church chaired.

The Church report concluded: "Many of the techniques used would be intolerable in a democratic society, even if all the targets had been involved in violent activity. But COINTELPRO went far beyond that. The program's unexpressed major premise was that a law enforcement agency had the duty to do whatever is necessary to combat perceived threats to the existing social and political order."

SHAKUR CLAIMED SHE was targeted by COINTEL-PRO, but the evidence is inconclusive. Evidence, however, does suggest she was targeted by another FBI investigation code named CHESROB, which according to Kenneth O'Reilly, author of *Racial Matters: The FBI's Secret File on Black America,* "attempted to hook former New York Panther Joanne Chesimard (Assata Shakur) to virtually every bank robbery or violent crime involving a black woman on the East Coast."

SHAKUR HAD THREE criminal charges against her dismissed, but her involvement with the March 25, 1977 shootout with police on the New Jersey Turnpike went to trial and had a different result. The trial of Shakur and Squire began on October 9, 1973, in the Middlesex County Courthouse, New Brunswick, New Jersey, amid extra tight security. The case received national publicity, and while awaiting trial, Shakur received mail from all over the country, mostly from supporters. Shakur responding by recording a taped message titled "To My People," which was broadcast on radio on July 4, 1973.

Calling herself a black revolutionary, which she said, "By definition... makes me a part of the Black Revolutionary Army," Shakur denounced what she believed was the "hypocrisy" of the U.S. legal system. She complained about the "double standard" justice that applied to blacks and whites and, which in her view, had made the judicial system racist. If convicted of the charges, Shakur faced life in prison. But she remained defiant.

"The pigs have used the newspapers and TVs to paint the Black Revolutionary Army as vicious, brutal criminals. They have called us gangsters... and compared us to such charlatans as John Dillinger and Ma Barker. It should be clear, it must be clear to anyone who can think, see, or hear that we are victims and not criminals."

Shakur and her followers complained about her treatment when she was imprisoned. In the foreword to Shakur's biography, Lennox S. Hicks, one of Shakur's attorneys in the New Jersey State trooper case, charged: "In the history of New Jersey, no woman pretrial detainee or prisoner had ever been treated as she was, continually confined in a men's prison, under 24-hour surveillance of her most intimate functions, with no adequate intellectual sustenance, adequate medical attention, and without the company of other women for all the years she was in custody."

Hicks would file one civil rights lawsuit after another on Shakur's behalf, complaining of the "barbarous treatment selectively meted out to her."

AT THE BEGINNING of the trial, Shakur revealed she was pregnant. The father was Fred Hilton, a codefendant in another bank robbery trial. The two had been placed in a holding cell to prevent their attempts to disrupt the trial. On September 11, 1974, Shakur gave birth in a local hospital to a baby girl she named Kakuya Amnala Olugbala Shakur. Shakur claimed in her autobiography that, shortly after she gave birth, several prison officers beat and shackled her for refusing a medical exam from a prison doctor. A mistrial was declared because of Shakur's pregnancy.

By now, the pressure of preparing for the trial created tension between Shakur and her aunt Evelyn, who had joined Shakur's defense team after quitting her professor's job at New York University Law School the day her niece was arrested. But Shakur fired Evelyn and was going to represent herself before they resolved their differences and once again began working together.

In his opening statement, Middlesex County prosecutor Edward J. Barone charged that Shakur had "executed" Trooper Foerster. Shakur was represented by radical lawyer William Kunstler who had defended a number of controversial clients in high profile cases, including the "Chicago Seven," who were charged with conspiracy to incite riots in Chicago during the 1968 Democratic National Convention. Kunstler argued that Shakur had her arms in the air when three bullets struck her arms and shoulders, and he brought to the stand forensic expert who backed Kunstler's claims.

The trial was a raucous affair, with the defendants shouting expletives at Judge Gagliardi. Shakur and Squire had to be put in a holding pen several times where they listened to the proceedings over loudspeakers. The two defendants were eventually banned from the courtroom and cited for contempt of court.

In her autobiography, Shakur described the trial's electric atmosphere. "The Kourtroom (sic) was placed every day with sisters and brothers who came to watch the circus… I had always said the best thing about being on trial is getting to see and smile at the spectators. Seeing so many beautiful people in the Kourtroom (sic) gave us the push we needed to get down and take care of business… Black folks had taken over the Kourtroom (sic), letting everybody know that they were watching what was going down."

In 1977, Shakur was finally found guilty by an all-white jury and sentenced to life in prison plus 26 to 33 years. To become eligible for parole, Shakur would have to serve a minimum of 25 years, including the four years she had already spent in custody during trials. Squire was also convicted and sentenced on murder and other charges.

TRYING AND CONVICTING Shakur was one thing; keeping her behind bars was another. She was now an icon for America's radical left, and the authorities feared, with good reason, that there would be an attempt to free her from prison. So they began looking for the right prison that would help keep her behind bars for life.

The authorities believed that the State Reformatory for Women could not hold her, so she was sent to the all male Yardville prison facility, where, as the only women inmate, she was kept in a special area staffed by women guards. Shakur's lawyers petitioned the court for a transfer to the State Reformatory for Women, but her request was denied. Then on April 8, 1978, Shakur was transferred to the Maximum Security Unit at the Alderson Federal Prison Camp in Alderson, West Virginia.

Shakur described the Maximum Security Unit, known at Davis Hill, as "a prison within a prison that had a stillness to it like some kind of bizarre death row. Everything was stale and dead."

Ten months later, federal authorities shut down the Maximum Security Unit at Alderson and transferred Shakur to Clinton Reformatory in New Jersey.

Shakur was incarcerated with some interesting radicals and criminals. At the Alderson's Maximum Security Unit, Manson family members Linda "Squeaky" Fromme and Sandra Good were locked up with members of the female wing of the Nazi Aryan Brotherhood, which was known for its attacks on black prisoners.

Shakur concluded that Good and Fromme were "clear out of their minds, fanatic in their devotion to Charles Manson," who, "if he told them to kill somebody, they would die trying to do it."

Shakur became friends with Rita Brown, a feminist, lesbian and white revolutionary; Lolita Lebron, a revolutionary involved in the struggle for Puerto Rican independence; and Mary Alice, a Catholic nun who introduced Shakur to liberation theology.

ON NOVEMBER 2, 1979, a man carrying false identification came to the Alderson Federal Prison Camp. Shortly afterwards, two more men came to visit a different prisoner. Remarkably, the visitors, who were believed to be members of the Black Liberation Army, were allowed in without being searched. The visitors suddenly pulled out a .45 caliber pistols, seized two guards as hostages, commandeered a prison van and headed for a visitor's area where Shakur was with the first visitor. Shakur, two hostages and the three BLA members got into the van and escaped through an unfenced section of the prison to a parking lot of the State School for the Handicapped, where they hopped into a waiting blue-and-white Lincoln and a blue Mercury Comet and sped away. Nobody was killed or injured during the prison break, but Shakur was now on the FBI's Most Wanted list.

"I couldn't believe that it had really happened, that the nightmare was over, that finally the dream (of escape) had come true," Shakur later recalled.

But she was not the same person who had gone the prison. She had changed in many ways.

"I was no longer the wide eyed romantic young revolutionary who believed the revolution was just around the corner. I was completely disoriented. Everything was the same, yet everything was different."

THE DETAILS OF Shakur's life on the run are sketchy. Shakur's autobiography does not discuss it and she has said little about it publicly. Authorities believe she was taken to a safe house in East Orange, New Jersey, where she hid for five years. The FBI circulated wanted posters in the New York-New Jersey area, but Shakur's support circulated their own posters that carried slogans of support. It is certain she had a well-organized network of supporters. For example, three days after her escape, more than 5,000 demonstrators organized by the National Black Human Rights Coalition carried signs that said "Assata Shakur Welcome Home." The FBI monitored the movements and activities of Shakur's friends and relatives, including her daughter, but got nowhere. FBI Director William Webster publicly complained about the lack of public cooperation. The stonewalling was understandable, given that racial tension the resulted after the FBI, in looking for Shakur, conducted clumsy and intrusive sweeps of apartment buildings in black communities.

In 1984, Shakur fled to Cuba and became one of 77 felony fugitives known to have been granted political asylum by the Cuban government. The fugitives included Robert Vesco,

Richard Linares and Victor Gerena who were wanted for or were convicted in the U.S. of murder, robbery air piracy and terrorism charges.

"Unfortunately, Cuba doesn't honor the extradition treaty that has been in place since 1940," Lt. Kevin Torney, chief detective on the Shakur case for the New Jersey State Police, told Fox News in 2008. "When the Castro Administration came to power, they no longer honored it."

Shakur was reunited with her daughter Kakuya, who had been raised in New York City by Shakur's mother. The Cuban government began paying Shakur $13 a day towards Shakur's living expenses and she went to work as an English-language editor for Radio Havana.

In May 2005, Castro called Shakur a victim of racial discrimination, claiming that the U.S. "wanted to portray her as a terrorist, something that was an injustice, a brutality, an infamous lie."

Shakur published her biography in 1987, but the tome contained little information that helped to clarify the events on the New Jersey Turnpike that had turned her into a wanted fugitive. In 1998, however, she granted an interview to the New Jersey-based WNBC-TV. Shakur, who was 50 at the time, told the television station that she had obtained a Master's degree, had written several books and had recently become a grandmother. She maintained she was not a murderer.

When asked by WNBC-TVC if she had killed state trooper Werner Foerster in 1977, she said, "I was in the car and I was told to put my hands up. I did and Harper started to shoot. And after that, everything was like fuzzy. It was horrible. It was like a personalized version of hell, you know, I felt like everything was moving around. My chest started to explode. My head started to explode. And the next thing they were coming by me and saying: 'Is she dead yet? Is she dead yet?'"

Shakur claimed she was still was afraid of the New Jersey State Police. "They want me dead."

The interview outraged the New Jersey law enforcement. Col. Carl Williams Superintendent of the New Jersey State Police in 1998, told the Associated Press, "I'm glad she's afraid."

Col. Williams denied that his police force wanted to kill Shakur, but stated, "We would certainly want to see justice done."

The Associated Press revealed that the year before, Colonel Williams wrote a letter to Pope Paul II asking him to raise the issue of extradition when he met with Fidel Castro.

U.S. AUTHORITIES CONTINUE to pursue Shakur's extradition and arrest. In 1998, a resolution before U.S. Congress called for the government of Cuba to "extradite to the United States convicted murderer Joann Chesimard (Assata Shakur) in order for her to complete her life sentence for the murder of New Jersey State Trooper Warner Foerster." In 2005 the U.S. Justice Department offered a reward of up to $1 million for "information directly leading to the apprehension of Joanne Chesimard (Assata Shakur)."

Although Shakur is currently residing peacefully in Cuba, a wanted FBI poster states that Shakur "should be considered armed and extremely dangerous." Shakur is still identified as one of New Jersey's State Police's "12 Most Wanted Fugitives." In May 2009, New Jersey State lawmakers announced that they were planning to introduce a resolution "calling on President Barrack Obama and Congress to pressure Cuba to return fugitive Shakur to the U.S."

Senators Sean T. Kean and Fred Madden also announced the introduction of a resolution calling on the U.S. to withhold normalization of diplomatic relations with Cuba until Shakur is extradited from Cuba to the United States. The senators said President Obama's move to ease sanctions against Cuba is an opportunity to bring back Shakur.

MEANWHILE, SHAKUR REMAINS an icon, not a criminal, to the radical left. On November 2, 2006, Mos Def Sonia Sanchez and the Malcolm X Grassroots Movement organized a Happy Birthday Assata Campaign, a national mobilization effort to commemorate Shakur's 60th birthday. More than 100 supporters showed up in the midtown Manhattan rally. In 2005, a "Hands off Assata" campaign was organized to "educate" the black community about Shakur's case. In the same year, several members of the New York City Council, along with black community activists, assembled on the steps of City Hall in Manhattan to condemn the Federal Government's $1 million bounty on Shakur.

Now in her 60s, Shakur still remains the defiant revolutionary queenpin. In a letter on her 60th birthday celebration, she wrote: "I am 60 years old and I am proud to be one of those people who stood up against the ruthless, evil imperialist policies of the U.S. government. In my lifetime, I have opposed the war against the Vietnamese people… the illegal coup in Chile, the invasion of Haiti and of Grenada and of every other illegal, immoral and genocidal war the U.S. government has ever waged. I have never been a criminal and I will never become one."

Most of America, however, would beg to differ with Assata Shakur's disclaimer.

EIGHT

The Black Widow

FROM THE 1960S to the mid 1970s, marijuana dominated the American scene as the illegal drug of choice. Much of the weed came from Colombia. But the situation began to change in 1978 when the United States began pressuring the Colombian government of President Julio Cesar Turbay Ayala to adopt a marijuana eradication program. Turbay finally relented, largely because he was accused of having links to drug traffickers.

Uncle Sam viewed Turbay's eradication program as a success, but as Damian Zaitch wrote in *Trafficking Cocaine*: "The impact of the [marijuana] eradication… perhaps diminished a supply whose days were already numbered… the Colombian drug traffickers had already found a more profitable product [in cocaine], easier to transport and with more promising results."

Kilos of cocaine were much easier to smuggle to the United States than the thousands of bales of marijuana that had to be loaded onto the mother ships or packed on planes and then illegally smuggled onshore into Florida. Moreover, the profit margin for cocaine was much higher. News reports in September 1978 put the cost of a pound of cocaine in South America at $27,000, about $35,800 a pound ($80 a gram) wholesale in the United States and nearly $290,000 ($640 a gram) retail.

Several of the Colombian criminal entrepreneurs who began entering the cocaine trade became members of the Medellin Cartel, the most powerful drug trafficking organization to emerge in Colombia in the mid-1970s. In the business sphere, the term "cartel" refers to a combination of independent commercial enterprises designed to limit competition. In the War on Drugs, the term is used to describe large-scale drug trafficking organizations, such as the Medellin Cartel.

The Medellin Cartel, named after the city of Medellin (population 1.5 million), the capital of Antioquia Province, operated until the early 1990s. The Medellin Cartel godfathers were known as "Los Hampones" (the Hoodlums) because of their backgrounds and rough criminal style. They came from the lower and blue-collar class and clawed their way up to riches using intimidation and violence. As cocaine became the drug of choice for millions of Americans, beginning in the late 1970s, the Medellin Cartel godfathers became fabulously wealthy; some of them even made *Forbes* magazine list of the world's richest people.

None was more famous than Pablo Escobar, the so-called world's greatest outlaw. Born in 1949 in Rinegro, a town located about 25 miles from Medellin Escobar had made so much money from drug trafficking by the late 1970s that he invested in U.S. real estate, including an $8 million apartment complex in Miami. Another cartel founder, the charismatic Carlos Lehder, was born in Armenia, Colombia, but was raised in the United States.

A bisexual with neo-Nazi sympathies, "Crazy Charlie" as Lehder became known for his unpredictable behavior, played a powerful role in pioneering an ingenious plan for smuggling cocaine shipments into the United States. Jorge, Fabio and Juan David Ochoa, brothers from a family with a long history of smuggling, joined Escobar and Lehder. Jorge, the oldest brother, was responsible mainly for turning his family business into a modern drug-trafficking organization.

AFFILIATED WITH THE Medellin Cartel, but a queenpin in own right, Griselda Blanco is another name to be added to the pantheon of major Colombian drug kingpins. Griselda had several monikers, including "The Godmother," "Black Widow," "the most bloodthirsty female criminal of our time," and the "Ma Barker of the Cocaine Cowboys." She is without a doubt one of the most powerful godmothers in criminal history, as well as the most brutal. Her violent crime spree, which may have resulted in 200 deaths in Dade County alone, is believed to have inspired the popular television series "Miami Vice."

"She lived to kill and it didn't take much of a reason for her to do it," explained Bob Palombo, a retired Drug Enforcement Administration (DEA) agent who for more than a decade played a key role in the investigation of Griselda Blanco. "She would kill those who were close to her and those whom she really didn't know. She left a bloody trail in Miami."

The Black Widow definitely did not need a good reason to kill. Jorge Ayala, one of Blanco's closest professional assassins, told the authorities in a sworn statement that she wanted Jesus "Chucho" Castro, one of her former enforcers, dead because he had kicked her son in the buttocks.

"At first, she was real mad 'cause we missed the father," Ayala said. "But when she heard we had gotten his son by accident, she said she was glad that they were even."

The Godmother showed no mercy for any of her victims. In another hit, the Black Widow was furious when she learned her hit men had killed a couple who owed her money but left their three children alive. Ironically, Blanco picked up the nickname

La Compasiva (the compassionate one) when she decided against using a machete to kill an arms dealer. The man pleaded with the Godmother to kill him instead with a gun that he had in his car.

Blanco kindly obliged, saying, "You see, I showed mercy to the man by shooting him."

Steve Georges, a retired DEA agent who investigated Blanco in the early 1980s, believes that the nature of Colombian society may have had something to do with Blanco's penchant for violence. "Colombian society is really macho, especially the criminal world, and it was really unusual for a woman to rise to such a high level in the drug trade," he explained. "Perhaps Griselda felt she had to be extra ruthless and vicious to survive and advance."

In her heyday, The Black Widow's style certainly caught the attention of the public. According to Guy Gugliotta and Jeff Leen, the authors of the 1989 book *Kings of Cocaine*, "By 1979, at age 36, she was the best known cocaine smuggler in the U.S."

The Black Widow is even more famous today, thanks to "Cocaine Cowboys 1" and "Cocaine Cowboys 2", two popular documentaries released in 2006 and 2008, respectively, and directed by Miami filmmaker Billy Corben. "The public found Griselda's story so fascinating that we did it in two parts," Corben said.

GRISELDA BLANCO GREW up in the slums of Medellin, Colombia, where she was abused as a child and forced to live as a street urchin. She survived as a prostitute before meeting her husband, Carlos Trujillo, when she was thirteen years old. Trujillo would father three of Griselda's children. Blanca was a big fan of "The Godfather" movie, and she named a fourth son after Michael Corleone, a character in the film played by Al Pacino.

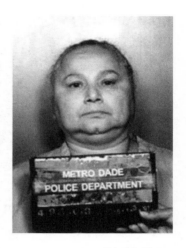

Blanco loved luxury. She reportedly purchased diamonds from Eva Peron, the legendary First Lady of Argentina, and owned a luxury penthouse on Biscayne Bay, a palatial estate in Miami Beach, and a fleet of exotic cars. A flamboyant character, even by the standards of organized

Griselda Blanco

crime, she loved to dye her hair and wear turbans, and as a powerful and sensual bisexual, she had no problem attracting the attention of either sex. She would often have lesbian and bisexual orgies, and she murdered strippers and topless dancers just for the hell of it. In the late 1960s Blanco and Trujillo immigrated to Queens, New York, where they launched a variety of criminal enterprises, including pick pocketing and document forgery (green cards, passports, and other identification papers). After Trujillo died of cirrhosis of the liver, Griselda flew to Medellin to be with a drug trafficker named Alberto Bravo. Eventually Bravo said something that offended Griselda, and she put a gun to his mouth and blew his brains out. The Black Widow ended up murdering two of her four husbands.

One of the Black Widow's seemingly unlikely relationships was with Charles Cosby, a mid-level drug dealer from East Oakland, California. "I was living my dream of hood wealth," Cosby explained in an article in the February 2009 issue of *Mids* magazine. "I had thousands of dollars, a nice car and a few fine

Charles Cosby and Billy Corben

bitches. I had the appearance of success. By no stretch of the imagination was I a kingpin. I was merely a face in the crowd."

That changed when Cosby saw a news report about Griselda Blanco and was "astonished" to learn she was "the Boss of Bosses" in the Colombian drug world.

According to Bob Palombo, Cosby became enamored with the Black Widow and wrote letters to her. "Griselda talked to him on the phone. She invited him to see her in prison. She made him into a bigger gangster," Palombo recalled.

Griselda and Cosby became lovers, and their story is chronicled from Cosby's point of view in the documentary "Cocaine Cowboys 2." "We weren't able to interview Griselda Blanco for our documentary, but we think the story of their relationship is accurate," said director Billy Corben. "There are hundreds of letters between them and photos in the courthouse that document the relationship."

IN THE EARLY 1970s Blanco became one of the first Colombian gangsters to see the potential of the cocaine trade, and she began to build a cocaine pipeline between Colombia and the U.S. cities of Miami and New York. Griselda's name is not normally associated with the founding of the Medellin Cartel, but she played an important role in its development, say law enforcement officials. For one thing, drug lord Pablo Escobar was most likely schooled by the older and more established Blanco after he entered the cocaine trade in the mid-1970s. Blanco also played an important role in turning the Medellin Cartel into an efficient money-making criminal machine.

"It's believed that Blanco was the one who went to the other major drug traffickers in Medellin—Escobar and the Ochoas— and got them together," Georges said. "She suggested they consolidate the transportation system from Colombia to the United States because trafficking cocaine individually drove up the cost."

Blanco liked to use female "mules" to move her drugs; she would have them wear the lingerie she designed in her Medellin boutique to conceal up to two kilograms of cocaine. By the time she moved to Miami in 1978, Blanco was making millions of dollars as the "Godmother of Cocaine." To protect her growing criminal empire, she organized a group of assassins in Miami known as the Pistoleros, who, after killing somebody, had to cut off a body part from the victim to prove it. Blanco is credited with introducing the motorcycle "assassin": a hit man who would ride past victims on the back of a cycle and spray them with machine gun fire.

Blanco used her wits to survive in the cutthroat world of drug trafficking. She once tried to fool a vengeful hit man by sending a coffin back to Colombia from Miami that was said to contain her body.

THE BLACK WIDOW became associated with an event, which, more than any other, signified the rise of cocaine as America's new drug of choice. The massacre happened in broad daylight on July 11, 1979, at Dadeland Mall, Florida's largest shopping mall in affluent Kendall, an unincorporated suburban community in Miami's Dade County. German Jimenez-Panesso, a prominent Miami cocaine dealer, and Juan Carlos Hernandez, his twenty-two-year-old bodyguard, had parked their white Mercedes at the Crown Liquors store at the southwest corner of the Dadeland Mall. Jimenez-Panesso came to buy a bottle of Chivas Regal, his favorite scotch, and when he and Hernandez strolled into the store, the clerk, Thomas Capozzi, who was standing behind the counter, directed them to the correct shelf.

The gangsters did not see the two bearded men who had gotten out of a panel truck in the mall parking lot. The two men strode into the store and, after spotting Jimenez-Panesso and Hernandez, pulled out their weapons—an automatic .380 Beretta pistol and an Ingram MAC 10 (Military Armament Corporation Model 10)—and opened fire, spraying Jimenez-Panesso and Hernandez with lead while smashing liquor bottles on the shelves. The firepower was awesome. Guy Gugliotta and Jeff Leen, in their 1989 book *Kings of Cocaine*, noted that the cops had taken to calling the MAC 10 the "Miami Chopper," and described it as a "Compact, box-shaped little black killing-machine that could send big .45 caliber slugs through a car body at the rate of a thousand per minute."

Hernandez died instantly; Jimenez-Panesso staggered out of the store with five bullet holes in him and died soon after. Capozzi was shot in the chest and crumpled to the floor.

Eighteen-year-old stock boy Morgan Perkins was in the back room, about to eat his lunch, when he heard a strange noise in the front. He walked back into the store and saw a bearded man in a white shirt and dark pants spraying the store with machine-gun fire. Perkins dove under the counter and scrambled on his hands and knees to the front door, trying to escape. But the hit men kept shooting, wounding Perkins in the ankle.

Pandemonium broke out in the mall. Women and children ran for cover as the hit men made their escape, still spraying the mall with gunfire as they fled. The manager of the beauty salon next door to Crown Liquors yelled, "Call the police, dial 911."

By now Capozzi had also staggered out of the liquor store and collapsed, but eventually he survived. Charles Diggs, the Assistant District County Medical Examiner who arrived at the scene, described it as a "holy mess."

"(Jimenez-Panesso) was trying to get out of the store," Diggs explained. "He was probably shot more than a dozen times. The liquor bottles were all smashed. There were bullet holes through the cases of liquor and wine. There were bullet holes in the ceiling and walls. He (Jimenez-Panesso) had four or five bullet wounds through the head."

Shocked witnesses recalled the indiscriminate shooting and the cold-blooded manner in which it was carried out. Some of them described the scene as being just like an Al Capone, Wyatt Earp or Elliott Ness movie. The killers left the Ingram MAC 10 inside the liquor store and the Beretta in the parking lot. The police found the hit men's truck two blocks away with the motor running and the doors open. On the sides of the truck was the lettering, "Happy Times, Complete Party Supply," and a phone number that the police determined to be fictitious. On the floor inside the truck lay six automatic weapons, with six bullet-proof vests hung in the rear. In inspecting the truck, the police found that the side panels were reinforced with quarter-inch steel and the rear doors had holes cut in them to accommodate the barrels of the killers' automatic weapons. The authorities described the truck as a "war wagon."

Miami police officers still marvel at what they had found. "We were still carrying six-shooters," Al Singleton, a retired Miami Dade police officer, recalled. "It was a real foreboding of things to come."

THE EVENT BECAME known as the "Dadeland Massacre." For Miami, the brazen killings were a sobering eye opener. As Dr. Charles Diggs put it, "We're talking about broad daylight in one of our busiest shopping centers. This is amazing. We're in the thick." The murders were the 161st and 162nd murders for Miami Dade in 1979. The killings had so overwhelmed the Dade County medical examiner's office that it had to add a refrigerator trailer to handle all of the corpses. Miami had never seen killing the way the drug dealers were doing it in the late 1970s and early 1980s.

The investigation of the Blanco organization continued, and by May 1984 the authorities believed that they had found the man who had gunned down German Jimenez- Panesso at the Crown Liquor store in the Dadeland Mall. He was Carlos Arturo Villegas-Hernandez, and they connected him to Blanco's organization. Villegas-Hernandez worked for Paco Sepulveda, the head of a faction within Griselda Blanco's drug trafficking organization. Panesso and another gangster named Carlos "Panello" Ramirez also headed factions. All three answered to the Black Widow, but they had become intense rivals.

"Panello ripped off Panesso on a 40-kilo cocaine deal worth $3 million," said Steve Georges. "Panello decided to go after Panesso before he came for him. He joined forces with Paco because Paco's girlfriend was sleeping with Panesso."

The gangster soap opera climaxed at the Crown Liquor store, where first Villegas opened fire on Jimenez-Panesso and Hernandez and then Panello finished the job. Government informants later told the authorities that Villegas-Hernandez felt "real good" about the killings because he had been the first to open fire.

By the early 1980s, Blanco's murder spree and her increasingly reckless behavior were taking its toll on her organization as well as on her personally. The Black Widow was never known for possessing self-control, and her increasing use of cocaine was fueling her paranoia. She murdered a niece of Colombian drug lord Jorge Ochoa, and the powerful drug lord vowed revenge.

To avoid the heat, Blanco fled to California in 1984 to hide and to tap into the West Coast's growing drug markets. Blanco rented a modest suburban bungalow in Irvine, California, for herself; her mother, Anna; and her youngest son, Michael Corleone Blanco, and she kept a low profile.

Finally in February 1985 DEA agent Bob Palombo and a team of fellow DEA agents tracked Griselda Blanco to Irvine, California, and staked out her home. One day Griselda's son Michael Corleone emerged and headed for the local playground, with his loving mother waving to him. When Palombo and his agents burst into her home, they found Blanco sitting on her bed reading the Bible. Palombo planted a kiss on the Black Widow's cheek as he always promised his colleagues he would do when he captured her.

"She looked at me as if to say: 'What the hell are you doing?'" Palombo recalled with a laugh.

The next day Blanco vomited on Palombo's shoulder in the back seat of a police car. "I think it was a nervous reaction," Palombo said. "Her arrest was finally sinking in. She knew it was over. She looked as if she was going to cry."

Blanco was held without bail and charged in connection with a cocaine trafficking case out of New York. A conviction in that case, and a guilty plea in a Miami-based trafficking case, would keep her in federal prison until the end of 1998. Meanwhile the wild and loco era of the Cocaine Cowboy had come to an end.

THERE WAS STILL to be one more remarkable twist to the Black Widow saga. By the early 2000s people who remembered or had heard of Griselda Blanco, the so-called Black Widow and Godmother of the Medellin Cartel who had terrorized South Florida in the early 1980s, probably assumed she was either dead or locked away for the rest of her natural life. So in 2004 it came as quite a surprise for many to learn that not only was Griselda Blanco alive and well, she was being released from jail.

It was a startling development, given Blanco's criminal record. She was largely responsible for the violence that made Miami the most dangerous city in America in the late 1970s and early 1980s. In smuggling millions of dollars worth of cocaine into the United States, she fueled the country's drug epidemic. She brought a gruesome style to murder and mayhem, and authorities linked her to more than 200 murders that included women and children.

In the early 1990s the state of Florida charged Blanco for having committed three contract killings in 1982. Two of them involved arranging the killings of drug dealers Alfredo and Grizel Lorenzo in their South Florida home as their three children watched television in another room.

In another, Blanco wanted Jesus "Chucho" Castro, a former enforcer in her organization, dead, but machine gun fire struck Chucho's toddler in the head as he rode in the car with his father. The Godmother could easily have ended up frying in Old Sparky (the nickname for Florida's electric chair), if convicted on any of these counts.

The star witness for the prosecution in their new case against Blanco was to be Jorge Ayala, a charismatic but ruthless psychopath in the mold of Griselda Blanco, whom authorities said was responsible for at least thirty murders. Ayala was one of the hit men in the three murders that Blanco was charged with masterminding.

BORN IN CALI, Colombia, Ayala went from being a car thief to enforcer to hit man in Blanco's criminal organization, earning from $20,000 to $200,000 per contract killing. In recounting how he murdered drug dealer Grizel Lorenzo, he told prosecutors: "She'd been shot in the chest several times and she's moaning. She is not dead; she's dying. But she's moaning real loud. I mean, real loud. I shot her two or three times in the back of the head. Right away she stopped moaning."

Ayala was a remarkably persuasive gangster, so convincing, in fact, that he could talk his way out of jail. In early 1988 he was awaiting sentencing in Chicago on a Fort Lauderdale bank robbery and machine gun possession charge when he convinced the Federal Bureau of Investigation (FBI) and the Chicago Police Department to let him out of jail so he could help them set up drug stings. Ayala managed to do this several times before he just walked away from prison. He was captured a month later in a small motel outside Chicago.

Ayala should have received a long sentence for his crimes, but the federal judge who sentenced him took into consideration his help in saving the lives of a U.S. attorney and his children. Ayala had heard that they were being targeted to prevent the prosecution of a drug trafficking case, and with the help of his brother Carlos, he managed to foil the plot.

The Ayala brothers supplied most of the evidence used to convict the three people involved in the murder plot. So instead of receiving at least a twenty-year prison sentence, Jorge Ayala received just six years. In 1990 the authorities transferred Ayala to Florida to face five murder charges in Broward County and Dade County. But he escaped the electric chair by agreeing to be a government informant. He gave depositions, testified in court, appeared before grand juries, and provided information on nineteen murders committed between 1981 and 1984. He talked about the Dadeland Mall Massacre and the war wagon that carried the assassins to the hit, a murdered man in a plastic bag dumped in a wooded area, a box containing a corpse in body bag that was found on the side of a Miami highway, and a hit in a Miami parking garage.

Prosecutors needed a conviction to keep Griselda Blanco in jail. Otherwise she would walk in year 2010 after completing her fifteen-year sentence. The prosecutors were confident that Ayala could spin his tales of the Colombian drug trade in court.

"He talks about killing like he is picking out cucumbers at Publix (a grocery store chain)," said Scott Sakin, a defense lawyer who was representing Blanco's codefendant in the murder. "It's chilling."

The prosecution had one problem though: Ayala's addiction to phone sex. Ayala had access to a jailhouse telephone and began frequent calls to the Major Crimes Unit in the Dade County Prosecutor's Office. Eventually the charming former hitman became friendly with at least three secretaries in the office. The Prosecutor's Office did not mind. They wanted to keep Blanco in jail, so they were willing to bend the rules to make their informant happy and cooperative. Ayala sent the secretaries money to buy him items such as tea, dental floss and newspaper subscriptions.

Fancying himself an artist, Ayala sent the secretaries pencil sketches of flowers and cute hand-drawn Garfield the Cat sketches. At times he gave the secretaries money to buy gifts for themselves. In return, arrangements were made for Ayala's wife to visit him in jail, where Mrs. Ayala got pregnant. The secretaries were smitten. One of them described the cold blooded killer as a "sweetheart." Another secretary arranged for a complete Thanksgiving dinner to be delivered to his jail cell. The telephone calls got increasingly friendly and racy and then downright pornographic. A staffer in the Prosecutor's Office who overheard some of the calls described them as "nasty."

One of the secretaries acknowledged that she had seen a photo of Ayala with an erection and had described it to other secretaries in the office. Complaints were made, and State Attorney Katherine Fernandez Rundle suspended the secretaries in late February 1998. Rundle also requested that a special prosecutor be appointed to investigate the allegations of impropriety. Florida's governor complied. The special investigator found that Ayala had made 451 phone calls totaling 168 hours from jail and that he had given at least $200 in money orders to the secretaries.

The secretaries were fired and a prosecutor in the Dade County Prosecutor's Office resigned after one of the fired secretaries accused him of sexual harassment, even though the prosecutor denied any wrongdoing. Secretary Sherrie Rossbach sued and had her attorney obtain a two-page sworn statement from Ayala in which he denied participating in sexually explicit phone conversations with her. He did, however, reveal that one of the other friendly secretaries asked him to get her a gun, which she wanted to use against Rossbach, and that another one of the secretaries had asked him for money to start an escort service. Ayala said he declined both requests.

Apparently some of Rossbach's allegations were so embarrassing that the prosecutor persuaded a U.S. District Court to issue a gag order and seal almost a third of the court document filings on the grounds that they might unfairly humiliate employees still working in the prosecutor's office. Meanwhile the Florida state attorney ordered a review of the procedures in the Major Crimes Unit. The recommendations included stricter supervision of staff members and new rules for using office phones.

THE SCANDAL COMPROMISED the Dade County, Florida case against Griselda Blanco and, given the embarrassing mess and the possibility that someone from her office might have had a personal relationship with Ayala, Prosecutor Rundle felt she had no choice but to plea-bargain with Blanco.

"The case got really screwed up," said Al Singleton, a retired Miami cop who spent years investigating the Black Widow. "It pissed me off. What happened was so embarrassing to the prosecutor's office that she just wanted the case to go away."

Blanco had been sentenced to three concurrent twenty-year terms on the Federal charges, one for each act of murder. But the actual time Blanco would spend behind bars for the three murders, though, was computed under guidelines in effect in the 1980s, when the murders took place. Under those guidelines, the convicted person had to serve only one-third of the sentence. Since Blanco had already served about four years, she would have to spend only three more years in prison. It was quite a deal. The Black Widow could be out of prison by 2001.

The U.S. authorities managed to keep Blanco in jail until 2004, when they were deported her to Colombia. Speculation abounded in the United States and Colombia that Blanco would soon be one dead Black Widow, given the trail of corpses she had accumulated during her criminal career and the people who wanted revenge for them. After all, three of her four sons—who had served time in U.S. prisons and returned to Colombia after serving their prison sentences—were murdered.

At the time of her release, DEA spokesperson Joe Kilmer said: "What she's got going for her is she never cooperated. What she doesn't have going for her is she gave orders that got a lot of people killed. It's going to depend on how long people's memories last."

Law enforcement officials who investigated Griselda Blanco said that she is the type of ruthless, cunning, experienced gangster who can survive in the cutthroat Colombian criminal world.

"Money is not an obstacle for Blanco," said Bob Palombo, the retired DEA agent who investigated the Black Widow for several years. "It can buy her a lot of things. I hear she's running with a bunch of hip-hop artists who are serving as her bodyguards."

Meanwhile Blanco's criminal legacy has given her a lofty spot in Miami's colorful and bigger-than-life rogue gallery of gangsters. It is a good bet that with time she will become as notoriously associated with Miami's gangster history as Al Capone was with Chicago's and John Gotti with New York City's. No doubt her infamy will only get stronger with time.

The two "Cocaine Cowboys" documentaries have made the Black Widow internationally famous, and she reportedly has sold the movie rights to her life story to Hollywood. This notoriety does not make the law enforcement officials who tried to put her away forever very happy.

"It's a bitter pill to swallow when I think of all the damage she did to Miami." Singleton said. "I'm sure Blanco is living off her fortune somewhere safe in Colombia enjoying life."

Only time will tell if the Black Widow will continue to enjoy a life of freedom.

Godmothers of Italy

FOR DECADES, THE women of Italy's La Cosa Nostra were content to stay in the shadows and play the traditional role of wife and/or mother, content and confident that their husbands, fathers and male relatives would shield them from their criminal activities. Still, if a Mafia man had to go to court, their wives would do their best to help them, even communicating with their lawyers, when need be, while they kept the home together.

Some women outside the circle of mobsters became more involved and worked as drug couriers, tempted by the money they could make. In May 1986, for instance, Vincenza Calli, the 40-year wife of Ignazio Mattioli, a janitor in a primary school and the mother of eight children, became known as the "heroin running housewife" when, on her way to New York, she was caught with heroin stuffed in her clothes. While her husband became near hysterical and started screaming while in custody, Vincenza was as calm as a solitary nun. In an interview, she explained why: "I saw how things were at once: bye-bye America. They told me they were amazed because I had stayed real calm. And what was I suppose to do if everything was over and done with?"

The status of the women of the Italy's Mafia's began changing in the 1990s when Italian authorities had much success in
busting many leading members of the major Mafia families and
either killing or putting them behind bars. A power struggle
within the Sicilian Mafia in the late 1980s led by Godfather
Salvatore Toto Riina and his subordinates led to the murder
of dozens of his rivals. A public outcry against this murderous
rampage, however, led to a massive government crackdown and
to the capture and arrest of Riina in January 1993. Even though
Riina's successor, Bernardo Provenzano, replaced the Mafia's
campaign of violence with one of Paz Mafioso, the government
did not relent, arresting Provenzano in 2006 after he had been
43 years on the run. In December 2008, about 1,200 Italian carbonieri, bolstered by helicopters, carried out a massive campaign
against the Sicilian La Cosa Nostra in Palermo, which led to the
arrest of 89 Mafia suspects. Basking in their success, the Italian
police boasted that they had "decapitated" the Sicilian Mafia.

In July 2010, Italy's 'Ndrangheta Mafia, arguably Italy's most
powerful crime organization, was dealt a major blow when police
arrested 300 of its members, including Godfather Domenico
Oppedisano. Robert Marconi, Italy's interior minister, described
the operation as absolutely the most important campaign against
the 'Ndrangheta in recent years.

The Mafia was no doubt weakened as much by their brutal
internecine struggles as by the government crackdowns. So it is
understandable that the power vacuum within the Italian Mafia
led to a growing number of women stepping forward to fill the
void and play important roles, serving not only as drug couriers
and helpers in the cutting and repackaging of cocaine and heroin
in their kitchens, but also assuming leadership roles, when need
be. This remarkable change is evident in the number of arrests

of women Mafia members. In 1990, just one Mafia women was indicted for mob association, five years later, that number had jumped to 89.

Some of the women were admired for their toughness and leadership skills, which earned them colorful nicknames. And so a woman shot in the face during a Mafia power struggle became known as a masculona, or tomb boy, while another woman gangster got the moniker of "la gattona," meaning fat she cat, as recognition that she was wounded in the shoulder during a turf war.

SINCE THE MID 1990s, the media has chronicled the activities of the numerous queenpins that have risen to power and grabbed the attention of an Italian public fascinated by the country's mob. In writing about the women in the Mafia, in her book, *Camorriti Politics and Bosses*, scholar Felicia Allum noted. "They don't find themselves on the margins of the 'Ndrangheta criminal world, in the shadow of their fathers, brothers, cousins, husbands, children and lovers. Over time, they have transformed themselves from being a part of a strong intimate support system into leading protagonists."

As for the Camorra women, Alum wrote: "Women take on active, formal roles in the Camorra, not only as directors of 'front companies,' but also in leadership positions, making strategic decisions regarding the clan's activities, taking matters into their own hands, even killing."

One such queenpin was Santa Margherita Di Giovine, known as "Rita," who got involved in criminal activity after she moved with her mother and many brothers and sisters to Milan. In 1993, she was arrested for possession of 1,000 ecstasy tablets. In a move that became familiar in Mafia circles, Rita ended up testifying against her entire family, including her mother.

Erminia Giuliano, known as "Celeste," for the color of her eyes, oversaw the financial interests of her mob-connected family, which included a chain of stores in Naples and the surrounding area and a franchise network of 56 outlets, not only in Italy but also in Tokyo, Bucharest, Lisbon and Tunisia. Celeste was a real prima donna. Press reports indicated that when the queenpin was arrested, she did not want to leave the house until a beautician was summoned to perfect her coiffure and dress her in a leopard skin coat.

Known as "the Black Widow," Anna Mazza became a powerful leader in the Camorra. As Roberto Saviano writes in Gomorrah, in the 1980s and 1990s, Anna's remarkable skills made the Moccia family into "one of the most important clans in the construction business; they handled contracts, controlled quarries and negotiated the purchase of land zoned for building."

Anna's husband, Gennaro Moccia, boss of Afragola near Naples, was murdered in 1976.

INTERESTINGLY, AS THE Italian Mafia women acquired power and garnered the attention of Italian authorities, they often went the way of their male comrades, turning into snitches. At age 23, Giancominia Filippello became the lover of Godfather Natale L'Ala, 47, and they remained so for 24 years. When L'Ala was killed in a Mafia war with the Campobello clan, Giancominia sought revenge by turning state's evidence against the Campobellos, but she had to go into hiding for her own protection.

When Carmela Minniti's husband, Nitto Santa Paola, was arrested in 1992, Carmela met with his lawyers and brought him information. When Carmela's two sons were arrested two years later, she broke down in public outside the courtroom and appealed for his release. That did not work, so Carmela became desperate and was about to become a snitch when a rival of her husband shot her dead.

TWO OF THE most powerful queenpins came from the Camorra and their criminal careers provide an up close look at how powerful women have become in Italy's La Cosa Nostra. The criminal careers of Maria Licciardi, known as "La Piccolina" because of her petit stature and Rosetta Cutolo, who has the moniker of "Ice Eyes," show that Italy's women gangsters could have formidable business and organizational skills and can hold their own in the macho world of Italian organized crime.

Maria Licciardi was born on March 24, 1951, in Naples, the home of the Camorra and Italy's thirds largest city, and grew up in a family of Camorra Mafia members. The Camorra, along with the Sicilian and 'Ndrangheta, are Italy's three major Mafia clans. The Camorra organized in the region of Campania and has traditionally financed itself through a range of criminal activities, from extortion to drug and arms smuggling to money laundering and illegal gambling. Mary's husband, Antonio Teghemie, was a Camorra mobster and her brother, Gennaro "the Monkey" Licciardi, became the supreme Godfather of the Licciardi-led clan. Gennaro, however, died of blood poisoning on August, 3, 1994, while in prison. One of Maria's two brothers, Vincenza or Pietro, would have assumed the leadership except they were either arrested or whacked, so Maria became Godmother by default.

MARY'S LOOKS BELIED her criminal talents. She liked to dress simply and looked more like a housewife than a godmother. In fact, she initially performed the role of a loyal, tight-lipped wife who cooked and cleaned and knew how to take care of the home, and might have continued playing that role except

Maria Licciardi

for the crackdown on Camorra Mafia during the mid 1990s. Maria's brothers, who were running the family business at the time, were imprisoned, and during the ensuing power struggle, her husband and nephew were murdered. With the male leadership in her clan decimated, someone had to take charge.

"Signora Licciardi is a true madrina (godmother)... absolutely," Stefania Castaldi, a Naples-based prosecutor who investigated organized crime, told Great Britain's *Daily Telegraph* newspaper in an August 2009 interview. "She was the sister of the boss, and she sat at the table with other bosses. She made decisions with them. She was right at their level."

Some criminologists believe that the role of godmother was not thrust upon Mary but actually happened by design. As Felicia Alum wrote: "Some believe that she became prominent because all the male members of her family were in prison, while others believe that Licciardi came to play a leading role in the Secondigliano Alliance (also known as the New Campania

Alliance), which organized to fight its enemies, to distribute profits among it members, to strengthen control over certain areas and to expand into others. What is true is that she (Licciardi) played a leading role in the Alliance and it activities. One has just to look at the number and type of bodyguards who protected her to see that she was not a nobody."

Yet, to stay in power as a queenpin was no easy task. In the patriarchal society that is the Cosa Nostra, Maria had to be on guard at all times and had to constantly prove she could lead. Enemies lurked and waited for the opportunity to do with her what they had done with the male members of her family.

Licciardi operated from a high rise in the Masseria Carbone district of Secondigliano, a strategic location from which she could view the activities of the entire district. She knew the Mafia's internecine wars were bad for business, and she reached out to rival Camorra clans and urged them to stop fighting for territory and power. There was enough money for everyone. So let us work together, was her message. The queenpin was convincing, and under her leadership, the Secondigliano Alliance agreed to make peace and became more organized and sophisticated.

Maria was as cautious as she was ruthless. For example, she never used the phone to communicate with subordinates, preferring to use short handwritten encrypted notes instead. She shunned the spotlight, too, although that was difficult for her to do because she was a woman. A lot of people depended upon Maria's clan for work, so she could count on them for their support.

"A big portion of the people protected them and worked together with them against the police," explained Luigi Bobbio, an

Italian prosecutor who investigated the Licciardi clan. "As soon as a woman takes charge, we can see that emotion plays a lesser part and that the organization reaches ever greater heights."

Once in control, Maria moved to expand the Mafia's operations. She may have been a woman, but she had had no qualms about moving into prostitution. As crime historian David Amoruso explained: "The Licciardi family had always stayed out of the business (prostitution) because of a code of honor, but with Licciardi that code was broken."

Under Maria's leadership, her clan forged an alliance with the Albanian Mafia to recruit girls to work the streets as prostitutes. It was a lucrative venture and the Licciardi mob was brutal in how it treated the prostitutes.

"Girls were put on drugs so they would not become an informant or run away," Amoruso revealed. "When the girls became too old, they were killed."

UNDER LICCIARDI'S DIRECTION, the Mafia expanded into cigarette smuggling, drug trafficking and racketeering. She used young drug dealers to sell heroin and cocaine in the neighborhood schools, constantly moving them from location to location so as to avoid arrest. The increased profits hauled in from the drug trade, however, came with a price. Indeed, it was the criminal activity that helped break the peace that Maria had worked so hard to establish.

An allied Camorra clan known as Lo Russo had a big disagreement with Maria over a heroin shipment from Turkey. Lo Russo wanted to sell the pure, unrefined and ultra potent heroin even though it could kill people and bring law environment breathing down the Mafia's neck. Maria's warnings were ignored and her worse fears were realized. People began to die on the streets (11 in April 2000 alone) because of heroin overdoses.

There was a public outcry, forcing law enforcement to come down hard on the Camorra. The fragile Maria Licciardi-built alliance fell apart and a clan war broke out.

The killing began in 2000, as Lo Piccolina sought revenge on those who challenged her authority. With 15 mob killings attributed to the Licciardi clan in June 2000 alone, it became clear to the authorities that Maria was intent on wiping out her opposition.

Sources acknowledge that circumstances dictated Maria deal ruthlessly with her enemies.

"Mary is too smart to go for pointless violence, which just begins the cops buzzing around, " said one Naples-based journalist who had watched the queenpin rise to power. "But when four of her people get shot on her own turf in less than a week, she had sent her hit men out to show she is not somebody who could be scared off."

THE BLOODLETTING, HOWEVER, lead to a massive manhunt for Maria in which had the police and paramilitary carbonieri swarming all over Naples. They did receive a tip that Maria was using her stronghold for a hideout, but they did not find her there. But the police did learn that Maria's mansion had marble floors, a grand piano and a Jacuzzi. Obviously, if the godmother had to hide, she was going to do it in style.

Grace under pressure would be the way to describe the queenpin's style, which explains why it was so difficult for the police to nab her. For example, police once stopped her at a check point and found a suitcase stuffed with 50,000 Euros. Cool and unflustered, Mary refused to tell the police what she was going to do with the money. They arrested the queenpin, but her lawyers secured her release and she went into hiding again. Now Maria was on the 30 Most Wanted Italians list and the pressure intensified. But rather than keep a low profile, she took the initiative and bombed the headquarters of the prosecutor, Luigi Bobbio as a warning to him—Back off!

Italy's godfathers had made this aggressive miscalculation before. In 1992, the Sicilian Mafia decided to send a message by eliminating the crusading Italian prosecutor, Giovanni Falcone, who was intent on breaking their stranglehold on Sicily. Falcone's long and distinguished political career culminated in the famous Maxi Trial (1986-87) in which 300 Mafiosi were convicted of serious crimes. The trail infuriated the Mafia, which warned Falcone that he was a marked man. The prosecutor took special precautions to protect himself and his family, but the Mafia still got to him, blowing up his car as he traveled on the motorway between Palermo Internal Airport and the city of Palermo. Falcone, his wife and three body guards were killed in the blast. Salvatore Riina was believed to be the perpetrator of the massacre and he had to go on the run. As we have seen, Riina was eventually captured in 1993.

The police manhunt for Maria Licciardi continued and 70 of her men were arrested. Maria evaded a police dragnet when police arrested another 13 of her lieutenants while they were hiding at a nearby rural farmhouse. But eventually the police discovered her hideout, and, on June 14, 2001, Maria was captured and taken into custody. She was considered so important and dangerous prisoner that she was put into isolation and her contact with the outside world severely curtailed.

But as Anna Maria Zaccaria, a sociologist at the Naples Federico II University, explained to the *Associated Press*: "She's in prison, but she still commands. Prison doesn't represent a barrier for the Camorra."

Maria Licciardi still remains behind bars but many Italians believe that she is still running the Mafia show.

ROSETTA CUTOLO (AKA Ice Eyes) was another queen-pin who rose to prominence in the wake of the Italian government's crackdown on organized crime. Unlike Maria Licciardi, however, Rosetta's exact role in the Mafia is unclear. Rosetta was the sister of the powerful Godfather Raffaele who oversaw the Nuova Camorra Organizzata (NCO), an organization he used to increase the power of the Camorra.

Raffaele often maintained that his sister knew nothing of the NCO, once explaining that: "Rosetta had never been a Camorrista... she only listened to me and sent a few suitcases of money to prisoners like I told her to."

Criminologists say that Raffaele's disclaimer is understandable, given the nature of the macho world of the Camorra. He could never be seen giving a seminal leadership to a woman, even if Rosetta was his sister.

Still, some authorities, as well as others in her own organization, questioned how big a role she played in it. As Italian law enforcement official Pascale Barra, said: "What have women got to do with the Camorra." But as Ice Eyes showed—A lot!

Scholar Felicia Alum noted that the role of the Camorra went through three stages during the period from 1950 to 2000. During the period 1959 to 1976, the women were a part of the Camorra support system. Yet, even during this early stage, Camorra women began to break away from the traditional form of behavior and display a voice independent of men. In the second stage (1976-1990), Camorra women were more aggressive in defying their men, although the media did not report this development. In the third stage (1990-2000), the women became criminals in their own right. This may be because they

Rossetta Cutolo

were no longer men in the Mafia who were suitable as husbands or because the women felt they had skills to be as good, if not better than their male counterparts. It was during this third stage that Ice Eyes emerged as a queenpin.

ROSETTA'S BROTHER RAFFAELE Cutolo was a powerful godfather, but he needed someone he could trust and put in a leadership position because he was behind bars for much of his life a mobster. The charismatic mobster was born on December 20, 1941, in Ottaviano, a municipality in the hinterland of Naples.

Raffaele was born to be bad. As a youngster, he committed petty burglaries, harassed shop owners and ran the street as part of gang of teenagers. Then he killed his first man and was sentenced to 24 years in the pen. Historically, prisons in Italy have been schools for the aspiring criminals, and Raffaele learned the criminal ways of the Mafia world. Given his dynamic personality and leadership skills, Raffaele organized a gang that became the nucleus of the NCO. When gang members were released, they took orders from Raffaele, and even though the godfather remained behind prison walls, he managed to grow a powerful criminal organization. Given his status as a powerful godfather, Raffaele had a variety of colorful aliases: "The Gospel," "The Prince" and "The Professor," among others.

By the 1970s, Cutolo had become so powerful he was able to control his prison environment to the point that he could make telephone calls to anyone on the outside and decide which prisoners should be moved to which jails. He took care of NCO member families while they were in jail, thus assuring their loyalty. Subsequently, the NCO organization that Raffaele built was described as the "most powerful organization ever to exist in the Neapolitan hinterland."

Such was Raffaele's power behind bars that he was able to get anything he wanted—even a color TV in his prison cell, where he dined on lobster and champagne. Later, in reminiscing about his life as a gangster, Raffaele said, "I don't regret anything about my life. Crime is always a wrong move. It's true, however, that we live in a society that is worse than criminality. Better to be a crazy man than to be a dreamer. A crazy man can be returned to reason. For a dreamer, he can only lose his head."

According to news reports, Rosetta had a love-hate relationship with Raffaele. Their lawyer revealed that they often had rows. "She thinks he talks too much. She wishes he wouldn't give interviews." She had no problem with giving her powerful brother this advice to his face. Some prosecutors even believe she was the power behind the family throne.

According to prosecutor Antonio Laudati, "Her brother had always been under the power of her powerful personality. He has been in prison for 30 years. During that time she became director of Nuova Camorra Organizzata in her own right."

ROSETTA'S APPEARANCE IS perhaps the big reason why many in the criminal underworld doubted her role in the NCO. Born in 1937, Rosetta was a gray haired frumpy looking spinster who loved to attend to her roses. She lived quietly in Castle Mediceo, and unlike her more flamboyant brother, Rosetta kept a low profile. So what woman could be more harmless, especially one who lived alone in a 16th century castle that was bought with money given to her by Raffaele and that had 365 rooms, a swimming pool and a large park? But the authorities later learned that the castle had become the headquarters of the NCO, where Rosetta held meetings with NCO comrades and visiting drug lords.

IT IS BELIEVED Ice Eyes assumed leadership about 1979 when the Camorra was about to break out as a power on the Italian criminal scene. As Raffaele's NCO grew, it began to seize the territory of other Camorra clans and was even was able to demand that those clans pay protection money if they wanted to stay in business. In 1978 another Camorra gangster Michele Zaza, a big-time Neapolitan smuggler, organized a rival group to oppose Cutolo and the NCO, but he had little success. Then in 1979, Zaza formed a new group called Nuova Famiglia, which was more powerful than Zaza's initial gang, and he was able to take on Raffaele's NCO. From 1980 to 1983, a bloody war raged in the Naples region that left several hundred mobsters dead and several thousand arrested. But the carnage intensified, even as the authorities continued to put the pressure on old Ice Eyes. In October 1981, Rosetta was holding a NCO meeting in her house when police stormed in. She barely managed to escape under a rug in a car driven past check point by a neighborhood priest. Rosetta went into hiding and was not seen in public again for ten years.

Still, she managed to direct the NGO's operations from a series of safe houses in various cities. Somehow Rosetta kept the NCO intact, even expanding its cocaine trafficking operation by skillfully negotiating deals with South American drug barons. In the late 1970s, Colombia had emerged as a leading distributor of cocaine, and its powerful cartels began to look globally for new markets. The Cutolos and NCO seized the opportunity. One Italian official said that Rosetta made frequent trips to Brazil and Venezuela and locations near the border with Colombia. In addition to her negotiating skills, Ice Eyes had a brilliant mind for numbers.

As the NCO fought to augment its power, the queenpin showed that she could be as ruthless and violent as any of her male comrades. She was charged with nine murders and narrowly failed to blow up police headquarters. Yet knowing that Mafia war was bad for business, she organized meetings to put an end to it.

Rosetta worked closely with Vincenzo Casillo, the NCO's second in command. Like Rosetta, Casillo was on the run after 1981 but managed to help to negotiate the release of Christian Democrat politician Ciro Cirillo, who the Red Brigade had kidnapped in April 1981. Casillo participated with Rosetta in many high level Mafia meetings to try to put an end to the bloody war. But on January 29, 1983, Casillo was murdered by a car bomb placed underneath the pedal of his car. Rumors circulated that Raffaele Cutolo had Casillo killed because he had stolen some ransom money from him, but Raffaele denied any involvement. Casillo's murder, no doubt, was a major reason for the downfall of the NCO.

ROSETTA MANAGED TO stay on the run as Italy's most wanted godmother until February 1993 when police finally found her hideout. Rosetta surrendered peacefully at an apartment in the suburban Naples town of Octaviano, a NCO stronghold.

She reportedly told authorities: "I am tired of being a fugitive."

By now, Rosetta had been sentenced to 9 and 1/2 years in absentia for Mafia activities and was wanted in five other cases, including kidnapping and murder. At her arrest, Italian police identified her as a NCO "mastermind."

By the time of Rosetta's arrest, the NCO was a shell of its former self, for many of its members had either been killed or arrested and those that survived joined other Mafia clans. Raffaele's power declined, and he lost much of his clout behind bars, as he was cut off from contact with the outside world. In 2007 Raffaele had a daughter through artificial insemination with a woman he had married in 1983. As a sign of Raffaele's declining power, authorities allowed Raffaele to see her for about fifteen minutes, but only after they searched the baby's diapers for weapons. In 2005 Raffaele asked for clemency in a letter to the Italian president.

"I'm tired and ill," he wrote. "I want to spend my last years at home."

But that is not likely to happen, for the Godfather is currently serving multiple life sentences.

MEANWHILE, ROSETTA'S NINE-year prison sentence was reduced to five years. In summing up Rosetta "Ice Eyes" Cutolo's role in the Italian Mafia, Felicia Alum wrote: "Rosetta clearly and intelligently looked after her brothers criminal activities. She was no substitute or bystander, but she was fully involved in the clan's activities and enabled it to survive while Raffaele was in prison. However, the clan would eventually be defeated. Rosetta demonstrated the limits of power connected to Camorra women during this stage (the third one) because the clan relied on her but did not want her to be seen as being involved or visibly active."

TEN

Mexico's Narco Drug Queens

I TALY IS NOT the only country where we are seeing increased participation of women in criminal activity. Take Mexico, for example. Perhaps more than any other country, Mexico has seen a surge in the number of women swelling the ranks of criminal groups during the early 2000s. The booming Latin American drug trade is the big reason for this development. The Mexican cartels rose to prominence in the late 1990s after the takedown of Colombia's powerful Medellin and Cali cartels, and since then, the country has dominated the Latin American drug trade. Today, Mexican drug cartels control 70 percent of the narcotics flowing into the U.S., which translates to an estimated $13.6 to $48.4 billion annually in illicit earnings.

Given the huge profits, rampant corruption permeates Mexican society, while the violence associated with drug trafficking has reached a crisis level, mainly because the Mexican government abandoned the passive stance it had adopted towards the country's drug cartels in the 1990s and early 2000s and went after them. Felipe Calderon, Mexico's newly elected president, sent 6,500 troops to the state of Michoacán in December 2006 to end the drug violence there. The result has been traumatic for Mexico. The country has had to deal with shocking assassinations that have included beheadings and other gruesome murders, raging gun battles, an epidemic of kidnappings and a breakdown of law and order. From Calderon's election to August 2010, Mexico's violence claimed more than 28,000 people.

And there seems no end to the carnage. According to the tally kept by the Mexican newspaper *Reforma*, the death toll for the first ten months of 2010 surpassed 2009's full year's tally by more than 50 percent.

MEXICO'S DRUG WARS have had a significant impact on Mexico's female population. In 2010, Mexico's National Women's Institute reported a 400 percent increase over the previous three years in the number of women imprisoned for federal crimes involving drugs and guns.

"The numbers continue to grow in spite of the violence we are witnessing," Howard Campbell explained to the *Dallas Morning News* in July 2008. Campbell did a study on women and the drug cartels in Mexico that was published in the winter 2008 edition of *Anthropological Quarterly*.

Why Mexican women are becoming felons is not clear. Some, such as Karla Robles, are entering the drug game because they believe they can make easy money. Robles thought working as a drug mule would be a lucrative way to support herself and her new born baby. A drug cartel recruited her because it believed that, given her gender and age, she would attract little suspicion at the airport.

"It was easy money and I enjoyed spending it," Robles recalled. "Shoes, clothes, bags, nightclubs... it just went." The young girl did not think of the consequences, and in December 2007, she was caught and sentenced to ten years in prison.

In an interview with *USA Today* on December 2, 2010, Luis Jorge de la Pena estimated that 40 percent of the women convicted of drug-related crimes were coerced to become drug couriers by their husbands.

"Normally, there were cases of women knowing what their husbands had done, but they were convicted as accomplices for not denouncing them," de la Pena explained.

One woman named simply Josephina by the Mexican authorities to protect her identity told police in Laredo, Texas, that she had gotten involved with the brutal Mexican paramilitary groups known as the Zetas when she 17. The Zetas, which are often identified as Mexico's most dangerous drug cartel, originally began as a private mercenary army for the Mexican drug cartels but have since gone independent to become a force in the international drug trade. Josephina trained in Zeta camps and she came to fear what the organization would do to her family if she ended her association with them.

"I would do whatever task was asked of me," the young girl revealed in the police video.

Other Mexican women have moved beyond working as drug couriers and have become actively involved in extortions, kidnappings and even assassinations. Eunice Ramirez had two jobs. By day, she would work as a hostess at corporate functions, political rallies and sporting events. By night, she joined a kidnapping group where she used her good looks to set up men for abductions. She kept this up until she was arrested in October 2010.

After competing in the Mexican beauty contest, Nuestra Belleza Mexico 2008, Laura Zuniga went on to win the coveted Miss Hispanic America in Santa Cruz, Bolivia. Later in 2008. Just months thereafter, however, Zuniga ignited a national scandal when she was arrested in Mexico for allegedly carrying illegal guns and about $53,000 in cash. Zuniga said she had been kidnapped by her boyfriend, Angel Orlando Garcia Urquiza, whom she identified as leader of the Juarez drug cartel. Laura claimed innocence when the authorities asked her if she knew anything about her boyfriend's illegal activities. Laura was dethroned as the Hispanic American queen, even though a judge found no evidence that she had been involved in criminal activity and released her from police custody in January 2009.

A FEW OF the female narcos have risen to the highest levels of the Mexican criminal world. These queenpins have a role model whose criminal career extends in time to the beginnings of the Mexican drug trade. Ignacio Jasso, AKA La Nacha, organized one of the first Mexican drug cartels in the 1920s, and operated a heroin business from her middle class neighborhood in Ciudad Juarez. Her main customers were heroin-addicted U.S. soldiers whom she serviced after ruthlessly eliminating her competition.

One report from a 1933 Mexican newspaper noted that: "La Nacha travels frequently through the streets in her luxury car that she just bought, and it seems she has some important influences and this why she has not been captured."

More recently, *The Newspaper Tree: El Paso's Online Newspaper* wrote that la Nacha was the first drug trafficker in Juarez to sell marijuana, heroin and cocaine.

"Her discreteness, good business sense and willingness to 'grease' the palms of government officials, allowed her and her gang to move about without having to engage in violent confrontations," the paper wrote.

Women gangsters like Maria Guadalupe, a native of Durango State, who arrived in Ciudad Juarez in the early 1980s, were inspired by Ignacio's career.

"The key is not to let any male dominate you, either in the head or in the heart. It's all business," Maria Guadalupe explained in an interview. "At least that's my philosophy, and one that I believe has kept me alive all these years."

Maria was an ambitious drug dealer who often represented the Juarez Cartel's interests in Colombia. The cartel operates primarily in the Cuidad Juarez-El Paso area, extending along the west Texas and New Mexico borders and into Arizona from Hermosito, Mexico. The cartel is one of Mexico's most powerful, controlling billions of dollars worth of drugs entering the U.S. from Mexico.

"I've never killed anyone," Maria said. "But that does not mean I'm afraid to use my .45. Don't underestimate me just because I'm a woman."

Guadalupe was part of the Quintero-Soto drug trafficking organization that trafficked in methamphetamine, cocaine and crack, moving the drugs from Mexico into the U.S., specifically to Phoenix, and then on to major U.S. cities, including Dallas, New York and Chicago. The organization also engaged in money laundering and bulk cash shipments by utilizing the secret compartments in vehicles to hide and ship money from the U.S. to Mexico.

On May 20, 2009, Guadalupe pled guilty to money laundering. Three months later, a U.S. District Court sentenced her to 37 months in a U.S. prison to be followed by three years of supervised release.

Enedina Arellano Felix, another queenpin, is allegedly one of the leaders of the Tijuana Cartel, one of Mexico's most violent cartels based in the Mexican city of Tijuana. Born in 1961, Enedina is the sister of former cartel leaders Ramon Arellano Felix (killed in 2000) and Eduardo Arellano-Felix (arrested in 2008). Following the murder of Felix and several of her other brothers, she became increasingly important in the Tijuana cartel According to the *Daily Beast*, an online publication, those close to Enedina describe her as reserved, calculating and highly intelligent. Enedina is one of 31 women on the list of drug smugglers sought by the DEA and FBI for extradition to the U.S..

MEXICO'S MOST POWERFUL narco drug lady is Sandra Avila Beltran, a striking brunette who comes from Mexico's criminal aristocracy and loves luxury and high fashion. The public has come to know her as the "Queen of the Pacific" in recognition of the important role she has played in developing drug smuggling routes along the Pacific Coast. In assessing Sandra's place among Mexico's drug traffickers, Patricio Patino, Mexico's Assistant Secretary for Public Safety, told *Newsweek* magazine: "Sandra's rise basically has to do with two circumstances: Her ties to a family that has been involved in drug trafficking over three generations, and a physical beauty that made her stand out as a woman."

The queenpin moved large loads of marijuana to the U.S. from Mexico that sometimes amounted to 15,000 pounds a load, as well as cocaine shipments as large as 700 kilograms. A U.S. indictment that seeks the extradition of Sandra to the U.S. details the movement of more than $20 million in U.S. currency into the U.S. and to banks in the Cayman Islands, as well as the acquisition of real estate holdings, in Texas and California, that include ranches, airstrips and residences.

Sandra has become so famous that her persona is now part of Mexico's popular culture. A band called Los Tucanes of

Tijuana has even composed a narco "Narco Corrido" folk song with lyrics that pay tribute to Sandra as a "very powerful lady" and a "big player in the illicit business." This Mexican ballad, focused on drug smugglers, has been compared by some critics to Gangster Rap. The lyrics of this "Narco Corrido" speak in laudatory terms of the drug smuggler's illegal activities, including murder.

Sandra Avila Beltran

One of the "Narco Corrido" songs pays homage to Sandra Avila Beltran as follows: "All the guests arrived at the mountain party in small private helicopters. Suddenly, they hear a buzzing sound and saw a chopper landing. The boss ordered everyone to hold their fire. Out comes a beautiful lady, dressed in camouflage and donning a cuerno (AK-47). Everyone knew immediately who she was. She was the famous Queen of the Pacific... the strong lady of the business, a true heavyweight."

SANDRA'S GREAT UNCLE is Jose Quintero Payan, a powerful Mexican narco who in June 2007 was extradited to the U.S along with fourteen other gangsters. According to the U.S. indictment, Quintero's drug trafficking operations span the area from South America and Mexico to the U.S. and the Cayman Islands.

Sandra is reported to be close to Ismael Mayo Zambada, a top drug dealer from the Sinaloa Cartel. The drug lord has made the *Forbes* list of the world's wealthiest and most powerful people, but he has had little opportunity enjoy his riches. Mayo Zambada remains a fugitive with a $2 million bounty on his head for information on his whereabouts.

In an April 2010 interview with a Mexican newspaper, Mayo Zambada admitted: "I'm terrified of being incarcerated. I think I would kill myself (if I was captured)."

Sandra is also the niece of Miguel Angel Felix Gallardo, a former big-time drug lord who is serving a 40-year sentence for the murder of a U.S. DEA agent, Enrique Salazar Camarena. On February 7, 1985, Camarena was kidnapped in broad daylight from near the American consulate in Guadalajara. The U.S. government demanded that the Mexican authorities find Camarena, but they resisted. So the U.S. Customs Service launched Operation Camarena along the Mexican border. Every car entering the U.S. was carefully searched for Camarena, the intention being to create bottlenecks on both sides of the U.S. American border and force Mexico's hand. When Camarena's tortured and bludgeoned body was found on March 5, 1985, he became the first DEA agent to die on Mexican soil.

Known as "El Padrino" (the Godfather), Felix Gallardo linked up with Colombian drug cartels and became the Mexican connection for the Medellin Cartel headed by the infamous Pablo Escobar. Felix Gallardo's arrest helped expose the widespread corruption in Mexican politics and law enforcement.

It is believed that Felix Gallardo's capture compelled Sandra to become a major player in the drug trade. She used her beauty and sex appeal to get ahead in Mexico's criminal world, but she also had the business savvy and the ruthlessness an aspiring queenpin needed to claw her way to the top. She spent a decade helping to forge alliances between drug traffickers in western Sinaloa State and those in Colombia, and along the way, she not only seduced drug lords but also corrupted law enforcement officials.

Her first husband was Jose Luis Fuentes, a crooked commander of the Mexican federal judicial police, who bore her one son. Fuentes called Sandra "My Queen" and spoiled her rotten by sending her on expensive clothing and jewelry shopping sprees to Puerto Villarta and other Pacific Coast resort towns. Fuentes was eventually killed by colleagues in the federal judicial police, and Beltran soon married Rudolpho Lopez Amavizca, another corrupt law enforcement official who headed Mexico's National Institute for Combating Drugs. Drug traffickers are believed to be responsible for Lopez Amavizca's murder in 2000 in a hotel room in the northern city of Hermosillo in 2000.

IN ADDITION TO her marriages, Sandra took on many powerful men in the drug trade as lovers. Her romantic conquests included such powerful drug lords in the Sinaloa organization as Ismael "El Mayo" Zambada Garcia, and Ignacio "Nacho" Colonel Villarreal Zambada Garcia, a former farmer who rose through the ranks of the Sinaloa cartel in large part because of his ability to bribe Mexican law enforcement officials and forge alliances with other cartels.

Zambada Garcia has been featured on America's Most Wanted, the program, which noted that the U.S. State Department is offering up to $5 million for information leading to his capture. Ignacio Colonel Villarreal smuggled multi tons quantities of cocaine in to Texas and Arizona during the early 2000s before he was killed on July 29, 2010, during a shootout with Mexican police. They found $7 million in cash in the house where he was killed.

SANDRA'S MOST IMPORTANT connection was Colombian drug lord Juan Diego Espinosa Ramirez (AKA Tiger)
with whom she got involved in the late 1990s. Sandra was a
good student and she listened carefully to the advice of her
Colombian boy friend. Sandra and Ramirez Espinosa used a
large network of women to bring suitcases filled with money to
Colombia and other destinations in South America to pay for
drug supplies. Espinoza Ramirez also helped the Queen of the
Pacific build her alliances so that she was able to control cocaine
shipments from the Valle del Norte in Colombia to the ports
of Western Mexico. Espinoza Ramirez was one of Colombia's
most wanted drug lords until his capture in Mexico City in
September 2007.

Sandra was a public relations genius who charmed her contacts in Colombia, but also showed that she could take care of
problems when need be.

Michael Vigil, a former head of international relations with
the DEA, told one reporter, "Sandra was ruthless. She used the
intimidation tactics of Mexican organizations." In other words,
the queen embraced the violence that came with the territory.

While moving cocaine from Colombia to Mexico, Sandra
also established a number of legitimate businesses to launder
the enormous sums of money she made from drug trafficking,
including a string of beauty salons and a real estate company
that handled more than 200 properties in Sonora State.

DESPITE HER LEGEND, Sandra managed to stay below
Mexican law enforcement's radar screen for a decade and avoid-
ed arrest, even though informants had implicated her in drug
smuggling activities early in her criminal career. Her fortunes
began to change in December 2001 when Mexican authorities

seized a tuna boat in the port of Manzanillo and found nine tons of cocaine worth more than $80 million. Cell phone records found on the boat tied Sandra to her Colombian boy friend.

The Queen of the Pacific was now a major target of the Mexican authorities who began scrutinizing her finances and business activities. Among other discoveries—the queenpin had laundered money through the purchase of 225 real estate lots, two houses and a tanning salon in the city of Hermosillo, Mexico. The authorities got a break in July 2002 when they detained two women who were carrying more than $2 million in cash. The women cracked under interrogation and provided valuable information that implicated Ramirez Espinosa and exposed Sandra's money laundering operation in Hermosillo.

The queenpin got another bad break when her son was kidnapped in the northern city of Guadalajara and the kidnappers demanded a $5 million ransom. Sandra decided to go to the police for help, but they got suspicious when they learned that the size of the ransom was $5 million. Who was this woman who could pay a ransom that large? Sandra decided to handle the kidnap negotiations herself, but the press got wind of the kidnapping and reported that Queen of the Pacific paid a $3 million ransom. Sandra said the ransom was less, but the kidnapping had given her a high profile.

The Mexican authorities were now hot on Sandra's trail. As a result of their investigation, Sandra was charged with conspiracy to traffic in drugs and money laundering. Meanwhile in Miami, Sandra was indicted on separate drug smuggling charges that U.S. authorities hoped would lead to her extradition. By now, the Queen had gone underground to avoid arrest, taking the name Daniela Garcia Chavez and living quietly in a middle class Mexico City neighborhood. Mexican authorities intensified their search and were able to track Sandra to Mexico City where they found that she was still maintaining her lavish lifestyle, driving a BMW, frequently dining at Chez Wok, an expensive Thai restaurant, and having her hands manicured in ritzy salons frequented by Mexican TV stars.

When 30 Mexican federal agents swooped in on a Mexico City diner to arrest the queen, they found her calmly drinking a cup of coffee. Wearing skin tight jeans and spiked heels, the queenpin asked the police if she could apply her makeup before they videotaped her being transferred to the woman's prison. In the videotape, she is seen smiling to the camera, walking downstairs on the arm of a federal agent. As two female guards handcuff her, she laughs and makes small talk. When the police interrogated her, she is seen on camera describing herself as just a housewife who made a little money "selling clothes and renting houses."

When the police ask why then was she in custody, she replied sarcastically: "Because there is an arrest warrant asking for my extradition."

Sandra was transferred to a Mexico federal prison in the northern Mexico City outskirts to await proceedings that the U.S. hoped would lead to her extradition.

At the proceedings, she told the judge: "I like to be called the 'Queen of the Pacific." And when taken away, she told the clerk of court: "Have a nice day."

On October 5, 2007, a Mexican judge ordered Sandra to stand trial in Mexico. She had no plans, though, to go quietly into the night. She complained about conditions at the woman's prison, claiming her cell had insects, or as she put it, "noxious fauna." She protested that the ban on bringing food from restaurants into the prison violated her rights. She asked guards for extra soap, her lawyers for extra makeup and prison authorities for extra time to put on the makeup before facing cameras. Sandra managed to wear figure hugging clothes, high heels and fashionable sunglasses. Obviously, Sandra was incarcerated under a different set of rules.

Julian Sherer, a Mexican journalist, arranged interviews with the imprisoned queenpin and published a biography about her. The queenpin even had several Botox injections to her face. Press reports indicate that the plastic surgeon was admitted to the prison by a person in charge of the medical area. News of Sandra's plastic surgery caused a furor, and the prison's director and hospital chief were fired, and an investigation launched.

In December 2010, a Mexican judge acquitted Sandra of the drug trafficking, money laundering and organized crime charges. Many observers were not surprised, given the corruption in the Mexican judicial system. But two months later, she was sentenced to one year in prison for illegal arms possession. Neither the Mexican government nor Uncle Sam were sure how the court rulings would affect the U.S. extradition request, even though Mexican law allowed suspects to be extradited to the U.S. even when they are facing trial in Mexico.

The story of the Queen of the Pacific still has no ending, but she clearly has become one of the most famous drug traffickers in Mexican history. If Hollywood has its way, Sandra Avila Beltran will soon become an international celebrity. Her life has already inspired a novel by Spanish author Arturo Pérez-Reverte Gutiérrez, which is being made into a movie starring Eva Mendes, Josh Hartnett and Ben Kingsley. Stay tuned.

ELEVEN

Mama San: Godmother of the Chinese Underworld

IN 1997, THE central government of the People's Republic of China's (PRC) central government ordered that a huge area adjacent to the city of Chongqing be incorporated into the city, and Chongqing became the word's largest metropolis with a population of 34 million. Since then, Chongqing has garnered a reputation as also being one of the world's most corrupt cities. So disturbing, in fact, has been the corruption that Chinese authorities ordered a crackdown on Chongqing's organized crime syndicates in June 2009. Indeed, it was the largest anti-corruption operation in the PRC since its founding in 1949.

Revelations about Chongqing's underworld, especially the activities of queenpin Xie Caiping, both shocked and titillated the Chinese public. Xie's trial revealed lurid details about sex and lifestyles and showed how deeply organized crime had infiltrated public life in China.

The high profile anti corruption campaign began in February 2008, when Cao Jianming, the Procurator-General of the Supreme People's Procuratorate, publicly expressed the Chinese government's determination to crack down on organized crime.

"The overall number of criminal cases keeps growing, demanding new efforts in maintaining social stability and harmony," Cao revealed. "We must handle all criminal cases endangering national security and social stability with an iron fist. Efforts should be made to resolve conflicts and disputes in a way they could be nipped in the bud early."

The *New York Times* agreed that the PRC had a big problem. "The CPC (the Chinese Communist Party) has been confronting many crises, but as a party, it is sandwiched by the two most serious challenges, corruption and crime," the newspaper wrote. It noted that while stability and order has been a top priority of the ruling elite, for the past three decades crime in China has grown much faster than its economic development.

It is difficult to fathom the idea that China could have an organized crime problem, given the authoritarian nature of the state, but China watchers generally agree that corruption forms the most formidable threat to China's future. One official has called the country's ruling body "one of the most corrupt organizations the world has ever witnessed." Meanwhile, economists have revealed that theft, bribery, kickbacks and misuse of political funds cost the state at least 3 percent of its GDP annually.

IN CHINA AND Chinese communities worldwide, organized crime syndicates are known as Triads and they have a history that extends hundreds of years in time. The Triads have an international presence, with members in nearly every country of the world. Their strongest presence, however, is in China, the U.S. and Southeast Asia. Like the Japanese Yakuza and the Italian Mafia, the Triads have well-organized initiation ceremonies and are involved in a wide array of criminal activities, from illegal gambling and human trafficking to murder and prostitution. In Chongqing, the Triad gangsters operate as well in a variety of legal businesses, such as the wholesale sea food trade, the private bus network, the taxi business and the entertainment industry.

Many of the Triad Godfathers began their criminal careers in Chongqing, where the city's top party leaders and government officials protected them for at least two decades. Corruption had been so entrenched in Chongqing that it took a directive from the highest level decision-making body in the PRC before enough law-enforcement resources could be mobilized to combat organized crime.

THE ANTI CORRUPTION campaign was led by the popular and charismatic Chinese Bo Xilai, the Communist Party secretary from 2007. Prior to the crackdown, Bo had repeatedly warned that the corruption threatened the CPC's legitimacy and public confidence in the political system.

Xilai is the son of Bo Yibo, an economic planner and one-time ally of the supreme leader Deng Xiaoping. In the 1990s, Bo was mayor of Dalian in northeastern Liaoning province before moving to Beijing in 2004 to become the nation's commerce secretary. In 2007 Bo was appointed party secretary of the booming municipality of Chongqing. The appointment was considered a promotion but many thought it was actually a sideways step. So Bo had to do something to bring himself back into the political spotlight, many China watchers concluded. Hence, the anti corruption campaign. By 2009, as his anti corruption campaign had gained momentum, Bo was being talked about as the future of the party. He had become a political star and a highly popular figure in Chongqing.

"He is trying to perform his way back to Beijing," Huang Jing, a professor at the National University of Singapore said. "It is a well calculated but risky gamble to get into the 5th generation (post 2012) leadership."

Bo publicly acknowledged the risk of a campaign that gave him a high profile and took on some of his city's most powerful political interests. But news reports indicated that Bo's crusade had the support and encouragement of the highest echelons of the Chinese Communist Party.

AND SO THE crackdown began in June 2009 when the Chongqing authorities began raiding the city's illegal gambling dens. Initially, the force involved 3,000 police, but the number eventually swelled to 25,000. The city police where re-assigned from their regular beat in order to break up any patronage that might have formed between the police and the Triads or corrupt officials.

By November, 2009, the dragnet had netted more than 1544 suspects, including some of the city's most prominent business-men and high ranking public officials. Bo's aggressive campaign, however, soon drew criticism. He was criticized for his style and personality.

In April 2010, *Asia Times* assessed that: "Bo, who trained as a journalist at the Chinese Academy of Social Sciences, had created a personality cult in Chongqing that some critics say harbors back to Mao Zedong and the Cultural Revolution (1966 to 1976). He has even claimed Mao as his spiritual mentor."

He was also accused of using questionable methods to get convictions. Lawyers for the defense claimed that they had not been allowed proper access to their clients, and that their clients had been tortured. Bo drew the wrath of the Chongqing legal community when he arrested Li Zhuang, a lawyer who was representing one of the Chongqing gangsters in the corruption trials. Li was accused of encouraging his client to lie, but Li claimed in court that police tortured him. It was to no avail. He received an 18-month prison sentence.

Xie Caiping

Mo Shaoping, China's most prominent human rights lawyer, charged that: "The case is a devastating blow for all lawyers. It is the basic problem that political might supersedes law and the rules."

INCLUDED IN THE arrests was 46-year old queenpin Xie Caiping, perhaps the city's most notorious gangster. Despite being the city's only female gang boss, Xie, who is nicknamed the "Mama San" of Chinese crime, was described as fitting the image of the tough, dangerous and hard bitten gangster.

One associate described her as :"Being good at debating and drinking, and very helpful to friends."

Given the tight control the Chinese authorities exhibited, the kinds of details that came out about Mama San and her activities were remarkable. Her trial exposed her incredible criminal career and the extent of the corruption in Chongqing. It also revealed her life of decadence excesses, depravity and sexual indulgence. So outrageous were the revelations that the court took on a circus-like atmosphere, as Chinese citizens flocked to the court to hear about the queenpin's salacious exploits.

A native of Chongqing's Ba-nan district, Xie organized a group of mobsters and ex-convicts who helped her establish an estimated 20 illegal gambling casinos, which generated hundreds of thousands of dollars in illegal profits before the crackdown. One of the gambling houses was right across the street from the courthouse. Many of her casinos provided free gifts to attract customers, while one illegal casino required customers to play with a minimum stake of $1,300 in local currency. At her trial Xie, denied organizing and paying gangsters and claimed the regulations she set for her clubs were "game rules," not "rules of the gang."

The queenpin employed a security force that kept an eye out for possible raids and operated like a legitimate police force. So even the police were not safe from Xie's displeasure. The queenpin's security once caught one police man named Xie Yingkuang, who was working undercover investigating Xie's gambling dens. In August, 2006, Xie's security exposed Yingkuang's cover. After being held for about twenty-five hours, Yingkuang was stuffed in a gunny bag and left in the wilds, many kilometers away from Chongqing.

On at least one occasion, Xie detained a police officer whom she claimed was a "thief from the outside." Xie was also said to have thugs beat up businessmen and women when they didn't agree to turn their establishments into casinos. The queenpin's treatment of informants was brutal. One of Xie's victims claimed at her trial that Xie ordered her subordinates to find out who reported to the police and then cut their hands and legs.

Xie used her wealth to live a lavish and decadent life style. She drove a Mercedes Benz, owned several luxury villas and kept a stable of 16 young men who provided her with sexual services. Xie tried to claim in court that she cohabitated with just one man: her driver, Luo Xuan, who was 20 years younger than her.

XIE'S WEALTH AND power allowed her to operate with impunity, and she was able to buy protection from the corrupt Chongqing establishment. For years, she was protected by her brother-in-law Wan Quiang, who until his arrest in June 2009 was the city's long-serving deputy police chief. During his tenure as a Chongqing's legal official and police chief, Wen was so busy acquiring the accoutrements of power that law and order in the city deteriorated. More than 640,000 criminal cases remained unsolved and 1,447 murders were not investigated. As the highest police official on trial, Wen's crimes were deemed so serious that he faced the death penalty if convicted.

The government had shown it to be deadly serious about the corruption campaign. At least seven people were executed in trials preceding Wen's. In 2000 a vice governor of Jiangai province was executed for taking $650,000 in bribes. Four years later, a former vice governor of Anhui province was put to death for taking bribes worth a little over $620,000. Both of these vice governors were accused of stealing less than half the amount that Wen was accused of stealing. Then the day after Wen's trial started, Yue Cun, a police official, was sentenced to death. Ironically, Caiping, Wen's most powerful gangster ally, did not face the same potential sentence he did.

Wen may have just been a public official, but the place he lived in was described as "palatial-like" with a two meter tall ivory screen at its entrance and at least one hanging light with crystal worth more than 100,000 yuan ($17,000) in his living room.

One investigator told the court: "I knew it (Wen's house) would be grand, but I never thought it would be that grand. We have retrieved a truckload of up-market luxury goods from Wen's house."

Wen was arrested and charged, but at his trial he denied protecting gangsters, claiming he knew nothing about what was going on in the casinos. Wen's lawyers even described the money he received from the others associated with the illegal venues as "gifts of relations," and Wen claimed he thought he was dealing with "businessmen."

Still the prosecution was able to prove that between 2003 and 2008, Wen received 786,000 yuan from mobsters, and that from 1996 to 2009 he received more than 15 million yuan ($2.2 million) in bribes from 19 organizations and individuals. Prosecutors were able to bolster their case when the authorities found $3 million worth of yuan buried beneath a fish pond on his property. The bounty received from payoffs included 181 bottles of choice wine, 80 pieces of jewelry and watches, 36 fine arts, nine cultural relics and 69 rolls of printings. Wen had a particular liking for Louis Vuitton belts and fossilized dinosaur eggs.

Wen was grilled on the witness stand for 70 minutes about the property. He claimed they were gifts he received on his birthday and other special occasions.

"That's normal etiquette and should not be considered bribery," Wen argued on the witness stand.

Prosecutors concluded that at the end of the day Wen and his family could legally explain no more then 4 million yuan ($680,000) of the property they received.

In testifying, Wen also tried to explain away his relationship with sister-in-law Xie Caiping. He claimed they were actually on bad terms; in fact, they did not even talk to each other. But prosecutors presented evidence that Xie often fled just before a police raid, sometimes with suitcase full of money, after Wen had tipped her off.

Given his power, Wen was use to taking what he wanted, especially women. He also had numerous affairs with all types of women, from college students to singers. The disgraced public official was also accused and later convicted of raping a university student in 2007 and 2008.

Wen's enormous sexual appetite helped bring him down. Fed up and in an effort to save herself, Wen's wife turned against him. The wife told investigators that from January to August of 2009 he was only home seven nights and each time he was drunk. Pouring it on for the prosecutors, Mrs. Wen gave her assessment of who was the most affectionate person in her family's household: the son, the dog and her husband—in that order. The prosecutors were unimpressed. The wife was charged along with her husband.

BY THE TIME Xie and Wen got to stand trial, nearly 6,000 Chinese officials had been charged with corruption. Wen was found guilty in May 2010 and Xie in November 2009. During her trial, Xie's behavior did little please the court, and her profanity laced testimony drew a rebuke from the judge. Yet remarkably, Xie's sentence was light, given the nature and extent of her crimes. She was sentenced to 18 years in prison and fined $150,000. Wearing an orange jump suit over a black t-shirt and baby blue prison trousers, Xie listened to the verdict without emotion. She was totally unrepentant. Meanwhile Xie's lover, Luo Xuan, received four-and-half years.

Outside the court, many in the large crowd were shocked and angered by the verdict.

"We didn't believe our ears when we first heard it's just 18 years," said Chen Yanling, a Chongqing resident who claimed she was beaten by thugs after refusing to turn her teahouse into a casino. "How many crimes did Xie commit?"

The written verdict noted that: "(Xie's) gang had practiced illegal activities, harbored narcotics takers and bribed public officials. This generated serious repercussions and greatly disruptive normal social lives."

Andie.com, a Chongqing web site, said that: "Xie and her gang had severely broken the norms of society."

Another onlooker commented: "Bear this in mind: She, to our great surprise, is the commander of an organized gang. I doubt if we can rehabilitate her within 18 years."

The big catch was Wen, and in April 2010, the state got what it wanted. The 55-year old disgraced ex-public official was sentenced to death for taking bribes worth more 16 million yuan ($2.4 million). The state, moreover, confiscated all of Wen's assets. Wen threw himself on the mercy of the court and admitted the charges, but to no avail. In May 2010, the appeal's court upheld Wen's death sentence. Given the Chinese government's determination to make examples, Wen's chances of escaping the death sentence did not look good.

Many of the 200 people, who gathered outside the courthouse, waiting for the verdict, were not happy with the ruling with what they considered to be a lenient ruling for Wen.

As a police van drove Wen from the court house, shouts of: "Kill him! Kill him!" were heard. But one woman told the *China Daily* newspaper: "I'm so happy the death of Wen is justice served. We are satisfied."

The Chinese government now had its biggest victories in their battle against corruption. The criminal careers of Xie Caiping, queenpin and Wen Quang, Chongqing former most powerful official, were history.

TWELVE

Australia's Crime Matriarch

IT WAS MARCH 17, 2009, and Desmond "Tuppence" Moran must have thought he was the luckiest gangster in the world. He had dodged an attempt on his life at his Union Road, Ascot Valley home in the northeast section of Melbourne, Australia. Moran had publicly claimed to be out of the criminal business, but the Australian police knew him as a member of the infamous Melbourne-based Moran crime family that had been involved in gambling, drug trafficking and other criminal activities.

The would-be assassins obviously did not believe him either. Moran was sitting in his car outside his home when a single bullet went through the front windscreen, struck the steering wheel and hit him as he sat in the passenger seat. Witnesses said that the hit man fled the scene after firing the shot. Remarkably, police told the press that they did not believe the incident was gang-related. Desmond's luck, however, ran out two months later on June 15 while he dined at his favorite café in Ascot Valley. Two men wearing balaclavas shot Desmond dead and then fled in a car believed driven by a third accomplice.

The killing of Desmond Moran was nothing new for Melbourne, for gangland mayhem had been going on in the city since the late 1990s. In all thirty-six reported crime figures were gunned down between January 1998 and April 2010 in what the authorities believed were tit for tat retribution murders, the result of various criminal families fighting for control and influence. In describing the carnage, journalists John Sylvester and Andrew Rule wrote in their book, *Leadbelly: The True Inside Story of an Underworld War*, that: "What has happened in Melbourne in recent years is unprecedented, a gangland war played out in public, whose participants have not hidden from secrecy but actually chase headlines. After each shooting, it was the criminals and their connections who held press conferences and the police who were reluctant to comment."

What was probably surprising was the person the police fingered as the mastermind behind Desmond's murder: Judith Moran, Desmond's sister in law. Those in the know said there had been bad blood between Judy and Desmond for some time over the fortune of Desmond's brother and Judy's husband, Lewis. Bertie Wrout, the man wounded when Lewis was killed in 2004, claimed that Lewis had stashed away a fortune.

"It's always over the same thing—money. Lewis was missing millions," Wrout explained to the press. "It's here, there, every-where. Various people were holding it for him."

DESMOND MORAN'S MURDER was the latest chapter in the remarkable life of Judith Moran, a woman who in her younger days was compared in looks to the beautiful blond Brit-ish actress, Diana Dors. The Australian press has dubbed her the "Crime Matriarch," a moniker Judy wore with pride.

"The media had made much of the matriarch label with which they tagged me, usually with negative connotations," she explained in her 2005 autobiography, *My Story*. "It is a label I have earned and must wear with pride because the fact is that to be a matriarch is to be a strong woman who truly cares for her family."

In her autobiography, Judith lambasted the press, accusing it of using the Moran family to advance their careers, and claiming that: "Much of the public vilification I have endured is because I am a woman."

Judy maintained she knew little about the activities of her husband, sons and other members of her family. "I'm really not sure what the media thinks I have done or have not done throughout my life," she explained. "Sometimes they have portrayed me as a kind of puppet master who has orchestrated deals and is completely involved in the underworld. I can say in all honesty that this is utterly ridiculous and could not be further from the truth. My role was always to be a caregiver and to make sure those in my life were looked after. As I have said, I learned early on not to ask questions."

The Australian public has found that explanation hard to accept, given the swirl of criminal activity clouding her life. Yet, she would not be the first queenpin to use her gender as a way of deflecting questions that might implicate her in criminal activities.

JUDY MORAN WAS born on December 18, 1944, the daughter of Oliver Ivy Brooks née McShanag and Leo Michael Patrick Brooks, in the tough inner suburbs of Melbourne. Her father worked as a flower seller and her mother danced in the Melbourne Theater. Money was tight, so to support his family, which included brother Brian, the father got involved in illegal activities. The father gambled as well as operated a business that sold watered down whiskey to unsuspecting visiting American soldiers. From Judy's early age, her parents' marriage was rocky, and when Judy was nine, her mother decided to leave the father and take her to Queensland, while Brian stayed in Melbourne with his father. Mother and daughter remained in Queensland for two-and-half years before moving back to Melbourne.

The parents tried to make a go of their marriage, but they split up again after seven months. To make ends meet, Judy's mother sold books door to door to various businesses until she became ill with bronchial pneumonia and had to quit work. At age 13, Judy left school to find a job. Meantime, dancing became Judy's passion in life and she worked hard to be a competitive ball room dancer. The young girl got so good at it that she began appearing on Melbourne television. She would work during the day and rehearse and perform at night. Then Judy met a young good looking man named John Cole who shared her affection of dance and fell in love.

Life was going well for Judy and her future looked bright, but she quickly learned that she could not take anything for granted, especially her health. One day, she blacked out while waiting for a tram. When Judy awoke, she found herself in the Royal Melbourne Hospital. Her health worsened and doctors told her that if it did not improve she would only have 12 months to live. Still, Judy's condition did not change John's feelings toward her. He gave Judy a diamond ring and at age 16 Judy was engaged.

The health problems continued. Judy learned that she had sarcoidosis, a rare blood disease and a mild form of leukemia. It took 12 years before she went into remission and was healthy enough to begin dancing again. The following year, on March 30, 1963, Judy and John were married. He had gone to work on the Melbourne waterfront where many of the major underworld crime figures got their start as members of the Painters and Dockers Union. Criminal activity centered around the control of the Union and the lucrative drug trade (primarily heroin and cocaine) that passed through the port. Judy got pregnant with son Mark Anthony but the marriage was not working out. John beat her and began to see other women. After Mark's birth, John moved out.

SHE MET LEWIS Moran and dated him for 13 months, Judy's experience with John soured her on formal marriage, so she decided to move in with Lewis but not marry him.

"Although I did feel uncertainty that I wasn't married, I didn't feel entrapped, as I had with John," Judy recalled. "I was able to cope because I still had choices and I could leave at any time. So I stayed because I wanted to."

Judy claimed she was shocked when she learned her husband was a pick pocket, and it was not until she found out Lewis had started an illegal book keeping business that she realized her husband was embarking on a criminal career.

"His (Lewis) father had been in the SP game for years, so he (Lewis) had a good idea how to run a business," Judy wrote in her autobiography. "He started up from home and eventually also worked from various hotels around the inner city. He had phones all set up on the distribution table and Lewis taught me how to take bets when he was working at the abattoir."

It was just the beginning. During the 1990s, Moran emerged as one of the Melbourne's major drug kingpins. Sylvester and rule write that Moran's criminal record "charts (Australia's) post-war criminal history. He was said to be involved in protecting backyard abortionists, SP bookmaking and steal-to-order break-in rings before moving into modern crime and ultimately drug trafficking."

Judy decided it was best if she stayed out of her husband business and focus on being a good wife. According to her, son

Judy Moran crime matriarch

John was about three years old before she suspected something was wrong in her marriage. One night, she followed her husband to her mother-in-law's residence and found him sleeping on a couch and with another woman. A heated argument ensued and Judy whacked Lewis on the head with a brass lamp. Lewis stormed out of the house only to return later, drunk. This time, Lewis brained Judy with a crow bar. It was the beginning of many trips to the hospital. Judy left Lewis, but he found her and begged her to come back. Family and friends urged her to take him back, too. Living on her own was tough, so finally, she relented to the pressure.

IN 1982, JUDY experienced the first of several tragedies in her life when her former common-in-law husband John was shot in the driveway of his Sidney home. After returning from John's funeral, Judy started receiving anonymous phone call. A man's voice asked her to put son Mark on the phone.

The caller said: "I am a friend. You should read about it in the papers and hear about it in the news. Your father's death will be avenged in two weeks."

Two weeks later, Michael Marshall, the man suspected in John Moran's murder was himself shot to death outside his home. The hit was part of a gangland war that had been raging since 1998 when Alphonse Gangitano was shot dead in the laundry room of his home.

Police learned that both Jason and his friend Graham Kinniburgh were in Gangitano's home when Gangitano's murder occurred. Kinniburgh's blood was found on a banister inside the house and pieces of his skin were found on a dent on the front security door. But police could not establish who had pulled the trigger. Kinniburgh remained under suspicion, but four years later, the coroner took Kinniburgh off the hook, finding that there was not enough evidence to positively identify him as the killer.

Known as "the Munster," Kinniburgh kept a low profile, but he was considered one of Australia's most influential gangsters and a mastermind of one the country's most successful criminal groups: the magnetic drill gang, which in one bank robbery alone netted $1.7 million Australian.

THE UNDERWORLD KILLINGS continued. One victim was shot outside his home, another murdered in a driveway shooting. Another gangster was ambushed by two hit men and killed in a car park. Still another was murdered with a single shot to the back of the head. Many of the killings remained unsolved, and they created a power vacuum within Melbourne's criminal community, as several gangs fought for control and influence.

Meantime, the problems for Judy's family mounted. One night, Jason and Mark were out at a disco with a group of friends when they got involved in a brawl. Both were arrested for assault and both pled guilty. Mark got four months in jail and Jason, five. Lewis continued to beat Judy so severely that she ended up again in the Royal Melbourne Hospital. The police wanted to charge Lewis with attempted murder, but she explained that she had fallen down the stairs. She left Lewis several more times but he would find her and convince her to come back. Often he would threaten Judy's family, so she came to believe that leaving him would be a more dangerous move than staying.

The last straw came when Judy discovered that Lewis was cheating on her with another friend. When she confronted Lewis, he went berserk and beat Judy one more time, putting her in the hospital again. She survived a punctured lung and a bout with tuberculosis. One day, after leaving the hospital. Judy tried to kill Lewis with a machete and then she went into therapy where she learned she had Battered Wife Syndrome.

If these were not enough problems, Judy had to deal with the deaths of the people she considered most important in her life: her mother and father. Both died within a day of each other during Easter 2000. The matriarch received another blow in June 2003 when she received a hysterical call from her daughter-in-law, informing her that son Mark had been shot and killed as he sat in his car outside his luxury Aberfeldie home. It was the third time within a year that someone she loved had died. At the time, Mark was firearms and other criminal charges. He, along with his brother, was also a major suspect in the non fatal shooting on October 13, 1999, of an alleged drug baron, Carl Williams, another incident in the Melbourne gangland war.

The police told Judy that Williams was a suspect in Mark's death, but she maintained she had nothing to tell them that could shed light on her son's murder. Again she claimed the ignorance of the gangster's wife who knew or saw no evil.

"I still don't know what went on that led to the murder of my son," she wrote in her autobiography. "I was his mother but he certainly didn't rush to my house every day to tell me all the things that were going on in his world. How many mothers know exactly what their grown children do every minute of the day, let alone who they associate with."

Like many of the gangland murders, Mark's slaying remained unsolved. It would not be the last for the Moran family.

JASON MORAN WAS also a big-time drug trafficker who was deeply involved in the Melbourne gangland war. Sylvester and Rule described Jason as a hothead who would act first and think later. Consequences were for others to worry about. In the Australian underworld, Jason became known as a "dead man walking."

According to the journalists: "Too erratic and too violent to be ignored, the drug dealer and suspected killer was always the popular tip to become another target in Melbourne's crime war."

Jason, in fact, feared for his life, and in September 2001, the authorities allowed him to leave Australia after he was released from jail for his part in the sports club brawl. He returned in November to give evidence for the inquest into the death of Gangitano. Not taking any chances, Jason reportedly changed addresses, moving to a luxury apartment in Grosvenor Park, Moonee Ponds, before settling into the home of a hotel owner friend. Jason went looking for unlicensed handguns for protection and was willing to pay $3,500 per weapon.

Unfortunately for Jason, he had one routine he did not change. He loved football and took his sons regularly on Saturday mornings to a football clinic, accompanied by his friend Pasquale Cameron "Little Pat" Barbaro. On June 21, 2003, Jason parked his blue Mitsubishi van in the car park at the rear of the nearby Cross Keys Hotel in Melbourne's Essendon North. It was 10:40 a.m. and the area was crowded with parents and children, a perfect cover for a man wearing a balaclava over his face and carrying a shot gun to make a hit and disappear. Jason was also carrying a gun, but the gun man caught him by surprise. The shooter blasted Jason through the closed driver's side window and then pulled out a handgun to shoot Pasquale. Moran's twin and his daughter were in the backseat of the Mitsubishi. They were among the five children who watched the double murder.

Homicide detective Andrew Allen described the shootings as a "gruesome and graphic scene." The children were described as "emotionally traumatized" and they were taken for counseling. A sawed off shotgun was found at the scene and a gunman was seen fleeing. A manhunt ensued but it was called off after several hours.

Again the police suspected gangster Carl Williams of masterminding the hit. He and Jason were believed to be involved in a war over control of the amphetamine industry and an alleged $400,000 drug debt. The bitter struggle had turned into a family feud. Williams' wife went to the police the previous year to complain that she had been harassed by Jason outside her children's school. She thought about getting a restraining order but withdrew the complaint.

Lewis was in jail but he was released on bail about a month after Jason's murder. Meantime, Judy began receiving chilling phone calls minutes apart, all with the same message. "We're going to kill you and Graham Kinniburgh."

IN DECEMBER 2003, Graham "the Munster" Kinniburgh was in the driveway at his home, parking his car, when he was gunned down in front of family members. He was carrying a gun and managed to get one shot off before dying. Judy described the family friend as thoughtful, not a hot head prone to violence as the press described and a man who had "the respect of everyone who knew him, and a few other besides." Judy claimed that Kinniburgh was killed because he knew who had killed Alphonse.

LEWIS NOW REALIZED it was only time before the killing machine came for him, too.

Yet, according to Sylvester and Rule, Lewis' friends said: "He was too stubborn to take notice."

Indeed, the police warned him he was next in line to be hit. Unfortunately for Lewis, he was just like Jason: Predictable in his movements. Lewis especially liked to drink at the same bars. So hit men had no problem finding him. In March, 2004, while he had a drink with his friend Bernie Wrout at the Brunswick Club, two men wearing the familiar balaclavas burst in shortly after 6:35 pm and shot them. Moran died on the scene, while Wrout was taken to the Royal Melbourne Hospital in serious condition but survived. Again, Carl Williams was the suspected mastermind behind the hit.

TWO WEEKS AFTER the death of Louis Moran, Judy signed a contract with the Australian celebrity agent Harry M. Miller to write a book that would, in her words, "Clear her estranged partner's name."

Under Australian law, it is a crime for someone to profit from writing and selling a story about actions for which they have been convicted. Up to that point in her life, however, Judy had never been convicted or charged with anything related to her family's alleged criminal activities. Still, the announcement for the book caused a public uproar and was denounced by the police, politicians and press and victims of crime. Noel McNamara, the President of the Crime Writers Support Association, described Judy's book as a "load of rubbish" and expressed concern that the book would make her "some sort of hero."

"Judy Moran is nothing but a gangster's mole," McNamara told the press. "Her two husbands were deviants and her two sons, cold blooded killers."

Moran defended her right to earn money from the book by claiming that: "Everybody has earned money off my family's deaths."

Later, after her book's publication, she claimed in an interview with the Australian television show, Current Affair, that she had not written the book for money, though she needed it.

In that same interview, she also gave a chilling but vague warning: "If it takes to the day I die, I will see you dealt with, one way or another."

Random House published her memoir in 2005. The press noted that the book was sparse on details of her family's crime world and provided mostly gossip about the family's personal lives. The book revealed little about Judy's relationship with Carl Williams, the man who had been implicated in so many of the Moran family killings, although she did talk about her poor relationship with Carl's wife Roberta, whom she described as being obsessed with the Moran family.

"The girls always knew that if they wear an outfit to a special occasion, Roberta would turn up next week wearing exactly the same outfit," Judy wrote.

Soon after publication of *My Story*, Random House had to recall the book and pulp 20,000 copies after it was found to contain false accusations with regard to a deceased police detective. The book was reprinted and delivered to the book stores in May 2005. Three months later, the book had sold 4,500 copies.

IN LATE MAY 2008, Evangelos Goussis, a 49-year old former boxer, was found guilty of murdering Lewis Moran. Goussis and two accomplices had accepted a $150,000 contract from Carl Williams and another man to kill Moran. During the eight week trial, Jurors saw footage of the murder in which balaclava-clad gunman ran into the club and chased Moran through a poker machine area. Lewis Moran cowered in the corner as the hit man shot him at close range. Judy Moran could be heard sobbing in court.

The evidence was based on the testimony of a career criminal who helped plan the murder and served as the getaway driver. The court kept his identity a secret.

According to the informant, after the hit, Williams telephoned him, saying, "Good one, mate. You have 150,000 reasons to smile."

Goussis was sentenced to life in prison. He won't be eligible for parole until 2039.

On January 29, 2004, Carl Williams was himself arrested for Lewis's murder. He was eventually charged with the murder of John and Mark Moran as well. Police believed Williams was responsible for about ten of the Melbourne gangland murders. In October, Williams was given a seven-year jail sentence to be served in the maximum security unit of Barwon Prison. On February 20, 2007, Williams pled guilty to the murder of Jason Moran, Lewis Moran and another gangster named Mark Mallia. In 2006, Mallia's tortured body was found stuffed in a wheel bin that had been dumped in a storm water drain and set afire.

MATRIARCH JUDY MORAN might have faded quickly into old age, except for the murder of Desmond Moran, and on June 16, 2009, Judy was one of three people charged with her brother in law's murder. Arrested with Judy was close friend, 45-year old Suzanne Kane, the sister of Trisha Kane and the wife of Jason, and Geoffrey Amour, whom the press dubbed Kane's "de facto partner." Detective Senior Sergeant Stewart Bales told the court that police had arrested Judy after she had disposed of the getaway car used in the shooting. Police also said they found three guns, a wig, two stolen license plates and clothing that matched those of the gunman.

In the aftermath of sensational killing, rumors abounded in the press about what happened. It was claimed that Judy was seen running to the murder scene crying: "Dessie, Dessie!" But sources close to the Moran family said Judy and Desmond hated each other.

Another source said Judy had been looking for two hit men from Sidney about six months before Desmond's murder. In a court hearing, electronic surveillance recorded a conversation in which Judy and Suzanne had allegedly told Amour they had to dispose or hide items used in Desmond's murder.

Still another report had Johnny whispering to the ashes of Lewis Moran, which were kept in her dining room: "I'm sorry, Lew." Many took this as Judy's apology for killing Moran.

During a bail application for Suzanne Kane, prosecutor Geoff Horgan told a hearing of the Supreme Court that phone records showed Judy had phoned alleged gun man Geoffrey Amour and told him, "Murder on." Horgan said this was proof that Judy was looking to kill Desmond.

Brian "The Skull" Murphy, a former detective, revealed how Judy hired him to investigate personal friends linked to investment properties she and Lewis had invested. After Judy had gone to the accountant who handled Lewis' money and he told her there was nothing left of Lewis' millions, Judy believed that the accountant was in a conspiracy with Desmond to "rob her blind."

"She didn't know why Tuppence should be controlling the money," Murphy revealed.

Judy had complained to friends of money difficulties and she did have to re-mortgage her home, but somehow she managed to go on a spending spree just weeks before Desmond's murder. She bought three luxury cars (Land Rover Discovery and two Chrysler sedans) in a thirteen-week period. The cost—nearly $200,000.

TROUBLES CONTINUED TO mount for Judy in the wake of her arrest. A suspicious fire in December 2010 nearly burned down her house. No one was in the house at the time of the blaze. The court, believing she was a flight risk, denied her bail three times. On her way to court for a pre-trial hearing, she claimed injury after being flung around in a prison van. At the time, she had a fractured hip and was in a wheel chair. Judy's lawyer, Jim Stavris claimed she was "forcefully" dragged into the prison van, which put her in an "extraordinary distressed state."

At the Dame Phyllis Frost Centre where she was remanded for trial, Judy claimed she had to do without shoes, did not have enough blankets because of a security crackdown and had not received her leukemia medications until 12 hours after she was suppose to take it. A corrections department official told the press that security at the facility had been increased so that the authorities could detect contraband.

In January 2010 she lost a vicious turf war in prison with Tania Herman, a woman inmate called "Muscles" and who was serving a 12-year year prison sentence for attempted murder.

One source told the Melbourne *Herald Sun* newspaper, Judy was getting too big for her boots: "She whinges like a stuck pig and was carrying on like she was queen."

IN LATE NOVEMBER 2010, Michael Farrugia pled guilty to killing Desmond Moran and agreed to give evidence in the murder trial of Judy Moran and other defendants. Given this development, the chances for the crime matriarch being found innocent and going home looked bleak indeed. Judy's continues to maintain her home as a tribute to the dead men in her life. On her dining table rests a big ceramic urn holding the ashes of her husband. In the backyard are floral tributes to Mark and Jason. After Lewis' death, junkies on orders of Carl Williams tried to burglarize her home, but she confronted one of them with a machete and they fled.

If Judy Moran ever leaves prison, she must live with the sobering fact that all she has left of her family are memories and monuments. The crime matriarch has shown, however, that she is one remarkable survivor.

THIRTEEN

Vonda's Gang

THE BOOBIE BOYS were one of Miami's most violent gangs responsible, according to the Miami Dade Police Department, for more than 35 murders and 100 killings over an eight-year period, beginning in 1993. The Boobie Boys were led by the gang's namesake, Kenneth "Boobie" Williams, who, from the late 1980s, built a drug empire worth an estimated $80 million.

Boobie was as ruthless as he was criminally entrepreneurial. Tony Monheim, a retired detective with the Metro Dade Police Department, recalled, "The Boobie Boys used AK-47 assault rifles in drive by shootings with the intention of killing off the competition. They created a terror wave in Miami for much of the 1990s."

In his book, *Street Legends*, noted crime writer Seth Ferranti described what it was like for the city of Miami during the Boobie Boys era: "It was a scary time for the community and police, with guns blasting ever night and bodies dropping. But it was also a time of street legends being born in a hail of gunfire."

What is not widely known is that the gang war involving the Boobie Boys was largely fought against a gang led by a queenpin named Avonda Dowling (AKA Jackson AKA Black Girl),

Kenneth "Boobie" Williams

which held its own against the powerful Boobie Boys. Dowling, prominent on the Miami drug scene for more than 15 years, raked in millions by selling both crack and powdered cocaine while killing scores of rivals and screw-ups who got in her way.

"When we began investigating the violence in Miami in the 1990s, we discovered Avonda was at the center of it," explained Jeff Lewis, a retired homicide detective with the Metro Dade Police, who focused on investigating the Boobie Boys. "We would bring in informants for questioning and ask them about Black Girl. We soon learned she was worse than Boobie."

Monheim conceded he was surprised to learn that a woman was leading one of the most active drug gangs in Miami, but as he investigated the Vonda Gang he began to understand why.

"She had an aura about her," Monheim explained. "People either respected her or feared her. Either way she was effective. When we brought people into our office for interrogation and asked them if they knew Avonda, they would say, 'Oh yeah.' But when we asked them if they would work for her, they would say, 'Hell no! She's dangerous.'"

BORN IN 1963, Avonda grew up the daughter of James Dowling (AKA Big Jake), a high ranking member of the International Longshoreman's Union in Miami. Police officials who investigated Avonda describe her as bright, tall, slender and athletic and, as sources pointed out, bi-sexual, with both boyfriends and girl friends.

Police records show that soon after graduating from Miami Carol City High School, Avonda began getting into trouble.

"She became a petty thief who would grab big-ticket items in the stores and then run out," Monheim explained.

Avonda was fearless and tough and, when challenged, did not back down from anyone. She was arrested for aggravated battery several times, beginning March 29, 1987. In a violent fight at 1140 Northwest 2nd Avenue, Vonda beat the victim with a bat, drove away and then came back to batter the victim with the bat again. Vonda was arrested in 1991 on two separate charges for fighting. In May 1992, she tried to run over a former employee after fighting with him. Through 1998, several more arrests followed for grand theft, aggravated assault and battery, obstructing a police officer, unlawful possession of a fire arm, driving with a suspended license, gun charges and cocaine trafficking.

Avonda got hooked up with a prominent Miami gangster named Bunky Brown. and rose quickly in his organization. In a prison interview in the Atlanta Federal Penitentiary in May 1998, Brown confirmed for authorities that Avonda bought drugs from him while he was in the business.

When Brown went to prison, Avonda took over his organization and got involved in crack cocaine trafficking. One of Avonda's top lieutenants, Jamal Brown (AKA Pookalotta), told investigators in December 2003 that sometime in 1994 a Haitian, by the name of Tony, taught Avonda how to turn powdered cocaine into crack. After much experimentation, she was able to cook crack in the pots on the stoves in the various apartments she rented.

Knowing how to cook crack gave the budding queenpin an advantage. After a few years, everyone knew how to cook crack, but by then she had become a bigger player in the Miami crack cocaine trade.

In 1992 Avonda married Jerry Jackson, who worked at the port of Miami prior to his incarceration for drug-related charges. The couple had two children, Jervante and Vonshari Hoardes, before divorcing in October 1992.

FROM 1985 TO 1999 Avonda maintained a so-called drug spot or "hole" at 11th Terrace and Second Avenue Northwest in Overtown, one of Miami's oldest and poorest neighborhoods. Initially, known as "Colored Town," Overtown is located between Northwest 8th and 20th streets and is bounded by I-95 and the Dolphin Expressway to the northeast, the FEC Corridor and Northwest 1st Avenue to the east and the Miami River to the southwest. Today, Overtown has a population of a little over 20,000 of whom 75 percent is black. Since the 1980s, the neighborhood has been marred by violence and a high crime rate.

David Gardey, a federal prosecutor who tried Avonda, told a Miami courtroom that the only things Avonda had for sale at the gang's drug store were crack and powdered cocaine.

According to Gardey, "Avonda's drug spot was the Walgreen's of cocaine; it was the Eckerd of crack cocaine—that is, the defendants operated their drug store 24 hours a day, seven days a week, preparing the packages of crack and cocaine powder they sold."

Avonda's spot occupied several apartments in one building. She used one apartment to stash her drug supply and another one for preparing the drug packages. Vonda's Gang had two types of customers: Junkies who used the drugs, and drug dealers who used the drug spot as a regular source of supply.

At any one time, Avonda had 10 to 12 people working for her, not including several chief lieutenants. Robert Lee "Rah-Rah" Sawyer was one of the queenpins' ruthless enforcers who would kill people encroaching on her territory. In December 2001, Rah-Rah testified before a grand jury that he first met Avonda in the early 1980s before the advent of the crack era. At the time, she was married to Jerry Jackson who was running a lucrative drug business in the Overtown area. Sawyer bought drugs from Avonda until his incarceration in 1985. Released in late 1986, he continued to make small purchases of cocaine. Eventually, Jerry Jackson went to prison, and Avonda took over his drug business.

Rah-Rah returned to the slammer in 1988 for cocaine trafficking. Then upon his release four years later, he returned to the drug game and bought increasingly larger quantities of cocaine from Avonda. On December, 25, 1992, Avonda threw a party in Rah-Rah's honor at her duplex on Northwest 50th Street.

Jamal Brown was another key associate of Avonda. Pookalotta told authorities he met the queenpin in the summer of 1993 through a mutual friend when he was 16 years old. He started working for Avonda as a street level dealer who received about $1,000 per week. Pookalotta moved into Avonda's duplex on Northwest 50th Street where she taught him how to cook crack cocaine and gave him other responsibilities. On January 1, 1998, Pookalotta was shot in front of his duplex. He survived but was paralyzed and confined to a wheelchair, unable to fend for himself.

"Eventually, Avonda got tired of taking care of him," Monheim revealed. "She no longer considered him a friend. She berated him as if he was responsible for his own condition and refused to do anything for him."

A third key member in Vonda's Gang was Andre "Bam" Mc-Whorter, who joined her in the 1990s. David Gardey described Bam as a gunman who worked with Rah-Rah to protect Vonda's Gang and its drug hole from competing drug dealers.

Avonda was a savvy business woman and an equal opportunity employer.

"She paid good money and had a lot of women working for her," Lewis revealed. "On a good day, a worker could make $15,000 to $20,000."

There was no doubt as to who was in charge of the gang. Avonda supervised the gunmen who protected the drug spot and the workers who packaged and sold the drugs. She was known to have personally distributed the drugs to the bigger customers at their homes or to a location where they sold drugs.

"We know that, at one point, Avonda personally delivered drugs to customers on a ten-speed bike," ex-cop Monheim recalled.

Avonda did not always sell drugs for money. On several occasions, she used the drugs to buy weapons, primarily AK-47s and MAC 10s. Just because the queenpin was a woman did not mean she shunned violence.

"She was ruthless, cold," Monheim said. "She had to be in order to rise to the level she did in the cut throat world of Miami drug trafficking."

THE FIRST MURDER police connected to Avonda involved a fight over drug turf. In 1986, a bold drug dealer named Michael McBride moved to set up his own drug operation in Overtown, right around the corner from Avonda's hole at 11th Terrace. McBride was an aggressive dealer, and to undercut the competition, he slashed the prices he charged for his drugs. Moreover, he sold a better quality drug than Vonda. So Avonda decided that McBride had to go.

Vonda Jackson

"In the cocaine business, a competitor is not defeated by better service, lower prices or a better product," Gardey told the court. "On 11th Terrace they were murdered, they were rubbed out."

Avonda hired Rah-Rah to kill McBride for $10,000 and half a kilo of cocaine. At around 11 p.m. on April 22, 1986, McBride was standing on the balcony of his apartment on 11th Terrace. McBride's apartment was close to Avonda's drug hole, but he did not realize the danger he was in. Rah-Rah killed McBride with a single gun shot, solving Black Girl's problem.

Avonda, however, was smart enough to realize that she did not always have to use violence to get her way with people. In December 2010, Calvin Bell, a high school football All-American who once worked as a bodyguard for Luther Campbell (AKA Sky Walker), told authorities about his relationship with Avonda. Bell became a favorite of Avonda after he stood up for her during a heated dispute she was having with a rival drug dealer and who was then knocked down with a rusty pipe. After that incident, Avonda catered to Bell and sold him crack at cut rate prices.

On December 21, 1995, at one of Avonda's parties at her house on South River Drive, Bell purchased one and half kilos of cocaine from Avonda. She began pressing Campbell to send "some chumps down," as she put it, from Daytona to buy drugs. Bell balked, concluding that she intended to rob and possibly kill the buyers. Bell got into a heated shouting match with Avonda and made the mistake of calling her several disparaging names before storming out of the house.

Bell returned to Daytona with the cocaine he had bought from Avonda. The next day, police served a search warrant at Bell's house and arrested him for possessing the narcotics he had acquired from Avonda. When Bell thought about his arrest, he realized that Avonda and her mother were the only people who knew he would be returning to Daytona. Avonda had set him up, Bell concluded.

AVONDA ENJOYED THE fruits of her drug trafficking enterprise. She was known for throwing wild parties at various locations, including the Omni Hotel and the Big House on Biscayne River Drive. The parties rewarded her loyal and hard working associates, as well as helped her court potential narcotics clients. Informants recall that the parties were lavish and extravagant and had every kind of drug one can imagine readily available. Huge mounds of powdered cocaine on silver trays were passed around, almost like hors d'oeuvres. Many of the parties ended in sex orgies in which partiers openly engaged in heterosexual and homosexual acts.

Avonda could be generous, too. At Thanksgiving and Christmas, for instance, she handed out turkeys to the Overtown community. When Roger Davis, one her top associates was shot dead at a gas station in Liberty City, the queenpin went the following day to visit Davis' mother to give her some money. Later, Avonda paid for the funeral. Vonda bought her father a house at 14641 Northwest 17th Avenue, which was valued at $350,000, occupied 4,119 square foot in size and had three bedrooms and three baths. Avonda's own house on 14750 South River Drive was 3,716 square feet and had four bedrooms, three and half baths and a pool.

Avonda was a big gambler who constantly played the numbers. In early December 2003, Pookalotta told authorities that on several occasions her winnings were more than $20,000. She seemed to win frequently and invested the winnings in her narcotics business. She also bought several expensive cars, including a Cadillac Escalante, Dodge Durango station wagon, Cadillac DeVille, Ford Expedition and a GMC pickup truck.

BY 1993, VONDA'S Gang was in a vicious gang war with the Boobie Boys, for Miami's drug turf was simply not big enough to accommodate the criminal ambitions of both Kenneth "Bobbie" Williams and Avonda "Black Girl" Dowling. While Vonda's Gang largely confined itself to Overtown, Williams built an empire that smuggled cocaine to 12 states through the Bahamas and Panama.

"The (Boobie Boys) Gang was truly a family affair," said U.S. Attorney Stacey Levine, who prosecuted the gang. "It was a very dangerous business and became more so as the Boobie Boys came into their own."

On the orders of Avonda, Rah-Rah, Bam and other members of her gang drove around Miami looking to kill Boobie Boys gang members. The Boobies retaliated in a tit for tat scenario. During a five-year period to 1998, Miami was paralyzed by the lawlessness of the gang war that left a trail of killings in some of Miami's poorest areas. The murderers wore ski masks, camouflage clothing and body armor and carried AK-47s. There were at least 62 shooting deaths and another 36 wounded during the period. Some of the victims were riddled by as many as 99 bullet holes and their faces were blown off.

"It got to the point that people were afraid to go anywhere," Lewis recalled. "Miamians became prisoners in their own neighborhood."

The killings began in earnest after the Boobie Boys killed Rah-Rah's close friend Wallace Fortner. On March 4, 1989, the Metro Dade Homicide Bureau interviewed Rah- Rah, who had agreed to speak to detectives about the gang shootings and drug-related crimes without his attorney present. Rah-Rah stated that shortly after the murders of Willie Geter (AKA Stinker) and E (real name unknown), he decided to go to Boobie's Christmas Party and kill him. They spotted one of Boobie's lieutenants instead and tried to kill him, but the lieutenant survived.

About a month later, Rah-Rah and an associate, Famous Johnson, were in Rah- Rah's truck near 99th Street and 27nd Avenue when they spotted three black males inside a small car. Rah-Rah recognized Marvin Rodgers, one of Boobie's close associates, as the driver. Then he saw that two passengers were wearing ski masks and realized Rodgers and his associates were looking to kill him. Rah-Rah fled the scene; the would be assassins circled the block looking for Rah-Rah and Famous. When it looked safe, Rah-Rah returned to his truck, but the police arrested him for leaving the scene of an accident. Rah-Rah was taken to the Metro Dade Police Department's Northside Station, but was later released.

Rodgers would not give up his quest to kill Rah-Rah, who had to be constantly vigilant to stay alive. Still, one day, he almost screwed up. As he backed a rented Lincoln out of a drive way at 590 NW 5th Street, Rogers and an associate named Fat Wayne ran up to the Lincoln and began shooting with rifles. Rah-Rah was able to speed away before anyone was hit by gunfire.

Weeks later, Rah-Rah told investigators, he was near his home at 95th Street and 26th Street driving a green Altima rental truck when he saw a brown and beige Honda Accord speed up behind him. Rah-Rah spotted Rodgers with two of his associates. Rah-Rah could see that Rodgers was carrying an AK-47. Gun fire hit Rah-Rah's car several times, but he managed to escape without being shot. Bent on revenge, Rah-Rah rounded up several of his friends to look for Boobie, Rodgers or any of the other gang members, but they could not find them. During the coming weeks Rah-Rah was shot at again. In September 1997, he was severely wounded while he traveling northbound on I-95 and had to be taken to the hospital. Rah-Rah claimed that, while in the hospital, his wife told him she spotted two of Boobie's associates in the hospital elevator and overheard them talking about trying to finish him off. Fortunately for Rah-Rah, nothing happened.

It was now a street war to the death, and with Rah-Rah looking for Rodgers, and vice versa. On December 31, 1997, Rah-Rah got lucky and spotted Rogers standing next to his car, talking on his cell phone, Pookalotta was driving the car and Rah-Rah and Bam were passengers. Rah-Rah and Bam got out of the car and approached Rodgers. Bam fired at Rodgers with his pistol, wounding him in the back of the leg. Sawyer then rushed up to Rodgers and fired his AK-47 into his face and chest. Rah-Rah and Bam dropped their guns and fled.

"I saw the photos of what happened to Rodgers and they were gruesome," ex-detective Monheim recalled. Police had no problem identifying the killer. "We discovered that Rah-Rah called Avonda right after the killing and that she paid Rah-Rah $12,000 and 1 1/2 kilograms of cocaine for the hit," Monheim revealed. "Then he fled to Tallahassee."

The day after Rogers was killed, Pookalotta was shot in the neck by a Boobie Boys gang in retaliation for Rogers' murder. The gunfire paralyzed Pookalotta and confined him to a wheelchair.

THE GANG WAR of attrition ultimately did in both Vonda's Gang and the Bobbie Boys.

"The war opened up opportunities for us because the public was outraged at the violence," Monheim recalled. "This led to the Feds getting involved, which was a good thing because the state didn't have the resources the FBI had. The Feds could use the RICO statue and also put gang members away on gun charges. The Boobie Boys went down first, but it took us a couple of more years to get Avonda. Meantime, unwittingly we helped her to move into Boobie territory."

More than 25 members of the Bobbie Boys were arrested, but Boobie, who was suspected in at least 15 murders, and some of his associates escaped and went into hiding. Before the trial, the *Associated Press* opined that: "The jury may need a guidebook to keep track of the defendants, witnesses and other players in the drug world who used their real names as well as nicknames and aliases."

The U.S. Marshals caught up with Boobie on May 17, 1999, alone and unarmed, as he left an apartment in a green Ford pickup he was driving under an assumed name.

"We had our men up there for more than a week, working around the clock, following up investigative leads," John Amat, a spokesman for the U.S. Marshals in Miami, said. "We did a traffic stop on him. There was no confrontation, no weapons found, and Boobie admitted to whom he was."

Kenneth "Boobie" Williams was sentenced to life in prison. Avonda was arrested, and on November 14, 2003, after a six-week trial, she was found guilty of narcotics conspiracy and sentenced to 20 years in federal prison. In a way, Avonda was lucky. The U.S. Justice system had considered seeking the death penalty for her, but John Ashcroft, the U.S. Attorney General, kept delaying the decision for months.

"In the end, he decided against it because there wasn't enough evidence for a death penalty ruling," Monheim recalled.

Rah-Rah and Pookalotta had already plead guilty. On February 2, 2004, Pookalotta Brown received a 25 year sentence. Rah-Rah, who had agreed to testify against Avonda, was not put on the stand. Still, he received 40 years on a plea bargain. They jury found Andre "Bam" McWhorter innocent of the charges.

The authorities had put Avonda and Boobie in prison, but did not find their money.

"They were really good at hiding it," Lewis said. "Boobie buried millions, while Avonda liked to hide her loot in Tupperware."

FEDERAL OFFICIALS LEARNED from several informants in prison that Avonda's drug dealing had not stopped behind bars. One informant, who was serving a 20-year sentence for conspiracy to distribute cocaine, reported that Avonda made numerous phone calls from prison phones to associates who took her calls at various pay phones around Miami. The informant stated that Avonda would use the code word "basketball" when discussing her cocaine deals.

Another informant reported that while Avonda was waiting trial, she was smuggling shipments of pot, heroin and crack cocaine to the Federal Correctional Institution at Tallahassee where she was incarcerated. The inmate claimed that she did not know how the queenpin was getting the drugs past the guards, but she and other inmates in the prison kitchen helped bag up the drugs Avonda later sold. The authorities also learned that Avonda was recruiting female inmates to help her in the drug trade when they were released from prison.

IN 2008, PRESS reports revealed that Avonda's son, Jervonte Jackson, was a star football player for Florida Atlantic University. It was great story and the press began reporting on the poignant mother-son relationship. Jervonte opened up to the press about his life and his mother, whom he defended and insisted had turned her life around before her 2003 trial.

"I know for a fact that my mother had stopped," Jervonte said. He revealed that his father had been absent from his life after he had turned two. "It was tough road," Jervonte conceded. "She (Avonda) did well, even though she did what she did. My mom was my motivator. She was in my corner... I'm taking small steps now. I can't rush it. I have training camp coming up, and I know me doing well in football will help get my mother home."

The following year, after signing with the Philadelphia Eagles, Jervonte continued to maintain that his mother had been screwed by the American justice system.

"They gave her too much time," Jervonte complained. "She got convicted for only having crack of less than 500 grams. They never caught her with this. This is something they put in her purse."

MEANWHILE, AVONDA MAY have her own plans for getting out of prison. She is currently serving time in a California prison, but was recently seen in Miami where it is believed she talked with authorities. For some sources that was a sign Avonda may be cooperating.

"That wouldn't surprise me," Lewis said. "I'm sure that, wherever Avonda is, she is up to her old shenanigans."

FOURTEEN

Gang Bangers from India

THE INCIDENT IS typical for rural India and one that has been playing out for centuries. The scene was a shack in the dusty and blazing hot district of Banda, a somewhat desolate region straddling the southern tip of Uttar Pradesh. Typically, a village in Banda is a cluster of whitewash mud houses built around a well, where the villagers have absolutely none of the amenities that we associate with civilized society. The district is marked by grinding poverty where the average worker makes less than a dollar a day, where children as young as six work, where corruption is rampant and where being a debit (an untouchable) in a rigid caste system is an immutable fact of life.

It is also a place where most women live in virtual bondage and where a poor woman has little hope for a chance at a good life and lives constantly with the chronic fear that she will be subjected to domestic and sexual violence. According to the United Nations, two out of three married women in India are victims of domestic violence and seventy percent of married women between ages 15 and 45 are beaten or raped. The Indian judicial system, moreover, is weighed against women.

As one website explained, "The male populations of these heinous crimes use money and muscle power to get bail, to destroy evidence and to continue to harass and rape women."

On this day, the woman who lived in the shack was, as usual, in fear of her drunken husband. The wife had married her husband before her teenage years, which gave him the right, he believed, to her as private property. He would take the daily reminder of his poor wretched existence on his wife by beating her constantly and without mercy and dragging her along the ground by her hair. The wife had taken the abuse silently, but, on this day, she had made the "mistake" of complaining to her husband that he was squandering the money meant to feed their children on booze. The brute went berserk; the physical abuse began.

The village knew what was happening. The young wife's relatives had tolerated the brutal treatment in the past, but on this day, Sampat Pal Devi, the wife's sister and neighbor, decided to intervene.

She went to the husband said: "Enough is enough. Stop it."

The husband was drunk, but his sister-in-law's demand still shocked him After all, women in the Banda district were to be seen and not heard.

He shouted angrily at Sampat: "Mind your own business!"

Sampat left but she was far from finished with the man. She rounded up five women from her neighborhood and marched to the abusive husband's house. They confronted him and began beating him with iron rods, walking sticks and even a children's cricket bat. They warned him to mend his bullying ways and treat his wife with respect.

THE HUSBAND COWERED; a movement was born. Word spread; other women in the region began coming to

Sampat with their complaints. Within months, a gang of women had morphed into the scourge of abusive husbands and corrupt public officials in the district.

"We are at the bottom of society with no help from any-one," Sampat told a Melbourne, Australia-based newspaper in December 2007. "We can't keep waiting forever. That's why I formed the groups so that the moment a woman calls me to say she's in trouble, we're on the spot fast. A woman on her own could never be effective. Men would just laugh at her. But when we are in a group, men get nervous. Even the local criminals are scared of us."

The group that Sampat organized was the all woman Gulabi Gang. Gulabi means "pink" in Hindi and refers to the sari, a sarong-style full length garment worn by Sampat and her fol-lowers.

Sampat has said, "We are not a gang in the usual sense of the term. We are a gang for justice. We wear pink because it is the color of life."

Since 2005, Sampat has gone from village to village in her region. belting out her collection of defiant protest songs against the established order and recruiting hundreds of poor illiter-ate females. No one knows for sure how many members the movement has, but within two years of the defining incident the number was put at more than 10,000.

Sampat's approach to women empowerment is both practi-cal and psychological She wants to teach her devoted gang members to read and write and to do math, but she also wants to teach them a skill so they can earn a living. Only then can the women be self-sufficient and free from the mercy of their families.

The Gulabi Gang has instilled confidence in the women who had joined the movement.

A 40-year old woman named Ratha, told one reporter, "Before I joined, I never went out of the house. Now I've tackled ministers and officials, and I've done away with my shyness and the veil."

The Gulabi Gang doesn't have regular meetings. Rather, Sampat and her followers walk with their lathis or sticks from village to village where they gather informally under a tree to discuss issues and problems. In keeping with her self reliance theme, Sampat has delegated leadership by appointing several women to serve as district heads for her organization.

Journalist Anuj Chopra wrote, "Moved by the deplorable plight of local women she became engaged with non governmental supporters to combat several malaises like arranged marriages and domestic abuse from alcoholic husbands, getting out of the house to interact with men, and relinquishing her ghunghte (Indian veil) was initially opposed by her family, but her zeal changed that attitude."

Men in Sampat's district have seen the power of the Gulabi Gang and have asked for help. Once, when farmers from the region took to the streets to demand compensation for failed crops, they asked the Gulabi Gang to attend their rally.

ORGANIZING A MOVEMENT like the Gulabi Gang is quite a remarkable achievement, given that its leader or queen-pin, Sampat Pal Devi, a native of Bundelkhand in Uttar Pradesh, is an illiterate sheep herder's daughter who, unlike her brothers, never went to school. Growing up, Sampat witnessed violence against women on a daily basis. Indeed, life is so dangerous for many rural women not just in Banda but other districts of India as well that they can not go to the outdoor bathrooms at night for fear of rape.

From an early age, Sampat rebelled against the repressive social order. When her parents would not let her go to school, she reportedly protested by scribbling on village walls until they relented. Sampat was just 12 when her parents arranged her marriage to a 20-year old man from a neighboring village whom he had never met.

A year after her marriage, Sampat bore her first child; yet, she has never accepted the traditional role of a rural Indian wife. After giving birth to two daughters, she wanted to be sterilized, but her mother-in-law wouldn't hear of it. In fact, the mother-in-law demanded that Sampat give her husband a son. Sampat eventually had six children but refused to veil herself in the presence of male members.

She eventually did the unconventional and found a job, working first as a tea vendor and then as a government worker until she quit because she did not find the work satisfying. She also served as a secretary for a non government organization (NGO), Adivasi Mahila Uthhan Samiti Tribal Women Development Society, which is based in Bichanda.

In June 2010, Sampat told the BBC: "I wanted to work for people, not for myself alone. I was already meeting with people, networking with women who were ready to fight for a cause…"

Helping the budding queenpin to achieve her goals was the fact that her husband did not fit the traditional mold of the rural Indian husband. He earns a meager income as fruit seller during the winter and as an ice cream during the summer months. The Pal Devis moved away from the husband's in-laws after they objected to Sampat's ways.

"They were against the woman of the house taking charge," Sampat explained. "We left their house in 1995. Despite pressure from my family, I got my daughter married after she turned 18." Sampat added proudly: "All four of my children went to school."

DESPITE THE POWER of the patriarchal dominated Indian society, the Gulabi Gang has no fear of challenging an entrenched corrupt bureaucracy and police force. In 2007, Transparency International, the German-based organization that monitors corruption word-wide, had India ranked 74th in the world for corruption, and it projected that India's poor would pay nearly $5 billion in bribes. In March 2009, 100 angry Gulabi gang members actually raided a police station and staged a massive demonstration to protest that the in-laws of one of the gang members had clicked photos of them as they made their way back to Bandi after attending a Woman's Day meeting. Gang members were furious that the in-laws would dare try to intimidate them. They only left the police station when a police officer assured them that he would take "prompt and necessary action in the case."

Sampat publicly warned, "If the police aren't going to initiate action against those who took out photographs with wrong intentions, we will come back again."

On another occasion, the Gulabi Gang learned that a government-run shop was illegally siphoning off tons of grain meant for the poor. So one night the gang stopped two trucks loaded with grain destined for the black market. The two drivers threatened gang members with knives, but the women vigilantes were not intimidated. They deflated the truck's tires and confiscated its cargo.

Gulabi Gang, a social movement

In Atarra, locals had been trying to get the village's pock marked dirt roads paved, but their pleas went unheeded. So in 2006 the Gulabi Gang invaded the office of the local magistrate and roughed him up

In another instance, the people of the Bandi district had no electricity for two weeks. During the day, they had to endure the intolerable heat, while at night they moved about in darkness. But one day, 100 furious women, all dressed in pink saris, swarmed the local office responsible for electricity. The boss had fled, but the gang made the staff phone him, demanding that he return to the office. When he refused, the women roughed up the staff, locked the office door and left with the key, vowing only to return it when the electricity was switched on. The locals got their power.

Gulabi Gang

Obviously, Sampat and her gang believe that to get a man's attention it sometimes is necessary to scare him. But to ensure they have the upper hand in the confrontation, they go armed with sticks and axes.

Yet, according to Sampat, "We don't have to use violence much anymore. Now just our name and that we are coming is enough."

GIVEN THE GULABI Gang's aggressive style and the fact that it has gained results, it is not surprising that the patriarchal Indian system has tried to criminalize the Gulabi Gang. Police have warned Sampat that they would not tolerate her gang taking the law into their own hands.

Ashutosh Kumar, Banda's Chief of Police, complained: "She (Sampat) is a bold woman but operates like a kangaroo court."

Kumar revealed in a press interview that the Gulabi Gang was under suspicion for having alleged links to Maoist rebels. Never one to back down, Sampat described the allegation as "garbage" and part of a conspiracy against her organization.

Following one police complaint, Sampat faced the prospect of being formally charged with offenses that included rioting, unlawful assembly, attacking a government employee and obstructing an officer trying to do his duty. Sampat said that she had not done anything wrong and that she had faith justice would prevail. So far, the police have not moved against Sampat.

SAMPAT COMES FROM a long line of prominent Indian activists who mobilized the masses into people movements.

These activists have been both violent and non violent in nature. The most famous Indian activist is Mahatma Gandhi, the pacifist who took on the British Empire, the imperial power that colonized India. Born on October 2, 1869, in the present day state of Gujarat, Gandhi grew up in a conservative family but became a civil rights advocate after moving to South Africa in 1893 to work as a legal advisor for a local Indian firm. Gandhi championed basic human rights for South African Indians before returning to India to become a leader in the struggle for home rule and an international symbol of non violence.

As an advocate of non violence, Gandhi was revered by his fellow country men and became known as Mahatma, which meant "great soul like a saint." In 1944, the British agreed to independence for India on the condition that Muslims and Hindus resolve their differences. In 1947, when the British allowed for the creation of India and Pakistan as separate states, rioting broke out between Muslims and Hindus in the new state of India. Gandhi was against partition of British India, but he fasted until the disturbances ceased. On January 13, 1948, however, a Hindu fanatic assassinated Gandhi. The death of the revered pacifist shocked the world, but he became a symbol of non violent action world wide and a role model for two revered leaders: South Africa's Nelson Mandela and the U.S.'s Martin Luther King, Jr.

MORE CONTROVERSIAL THAN the nonviolent legacy of Mahatma Gandhi was the remarkable life and times of Phoolan Devi, the so-called Bandit Queen of India. Phoolan became a Robin Hood like figure to her supporters, robbing the rich people of the upper caste for the benefit of the poor.

Journalist Anthony Bruno described the role she played: "Phoolan Devi was unique. She was an idealist who sought to right the wrongs of society and who saw banditry as a way to correct social inequality by toppling the oppressors and redistributing their wealth."

To the establishment and her bitter enemies, on the other hand, the Bandit Queen was a ruthless, common criminal who perpetuated one of the largest gang massacres in India's history.

Phoolan came from the Bundelkhand, the same region that produced Sampat Devi Pal and her Gulag Gang members. The region has a long history of Dacoit gangs who preyed on travelers, looted villages and killed its enemies without mercy. Ironically, despite Phoolan's violent and ruthless legacy, Gandhi became one of her main sources of inspiration.

Phoolan Devi was born in 1963 in the village Gorha Ka Purwa in Utter Pradesh, the second child in a family of four sisters and a younger brother. The family was poor but not the poorest in the village, evident by the fact that the family owned an acre of land that had a huge neem tree growing on it. From an early age Phoolan showed herself to be stubborn, fearless and head strong, even though she was born into the lower castes and came from a patriarchal society. At age 10, she bathed nude in a river in broad daylight, unconcerned that somebody may be watching here. The consequence was an underserved reputation for promiscuity.

When Phoolan's cousin, Mayadin, cheated her father by cutting down his prize neem tree and selling the wood, and the father did nothing, Phoolan confronted Mayadin and demanded he compensate her father. Mayadin tried to ignore her, but Phoolan persisted. She even taunted him in public before he hit her with a brick. The bold 10-year old child continued to harangue her cousin until he tried to get rid of her by forcing her to marry a man in his thirties, who lived many miles away.

Phoolan reputation for promiscuity proved to be untrue. She was still a virgin, evident later when she revealed that she feared his "snake," as she called his penis, and refused to have sex with him. Then she did the unthinkable for a woman of her low caste and position in society. She left her husband and made the long walk home. Phoolan's mother was so embarrassed by her daughter's action that she urged Phoolan to jump in the well and kill herself. Phoolan took Mayadin to court instead.

The system, however, was weighted against Phoolan, and the police arrested her after Mayadin accused her of stealing from his house. She was thrown in a rat-infested cell and beaten and raped repeatedly. The horrible experience failed to break the young girl's spirit, but by now, her reputation for impertinence had spread beyond her village. Then a gang of robbers led by the notorious Babu Gujar showed up at Phoolan's village and threatened to kidnap Phoolan and cut off her nose, a traditional Indian punishment for women who did not keep their place. It is not clear how it happened, but Phoolan was kidnapped and brought to Gujar who, along with his men, raped and abused her for three days.

Unfortunately for Gujar, his chief lieutenant, Vikram Mallah had become a secret admirer of Phoolan. Unable to accept the abuse against Phoolan any longer, Mallah shot and killed Gujar. Because of her brutal experiences at the hands of men, Phoolan had come to distrust and hate them, but she fell for Vikram, grateful for what he had done for her.

In her autobiography, Phoolan recalled: "I felt strange—happy but still frightened. A man had touched me softly, he had stroked my hair and touched my cheeks. I felt I could trust him, something I had never felt about a stranger or a man before.

Gradually, I stopped sobbing, and my tears dried. If I stayed with him, perhaps I would be happy, no more beatings, no more pain, no more humiliation."

VIKRAM TAUGHT PHOOLAN in the ways of dacoit (bandit)—how to dress, use a rifle, steal, kidnap and even kill. Phoolan was slight and a mere 5 feet tall, but she garnered a towering reputation.

In an article for Trutv.com, writer Anthony Bruno described her appearance: "Phoolan often wore military style Khaki jacket, denim jeans and zippered boots. Her dark, straight hair was cut short ending at the neck. By some accounts she wore lipstick and red nail polish. A wide red bandanna—the spirit of vengeance—was tied around her head, covering her hairline and brows. She carried a stern gun and a bandolier across her chest."

The Bandit Queen and her lover became the Bonnie and Clyde of rural northern India.

Phoolan described her life as a dacoit in an interview with one media source as follows: "Once I became a dacoit and started making lists of people who had tortured me, who had abused me, I was able to pay them back in kind, and it pleased me tremendously when they were brought before me and fell at my feet to pay obeisance to me. I was happy most of the time that I was a dacoit (but) being a dacoit was a hard life. We'd go from one state to another, walking the entire night. Then we'd have to survey the area, pay our informers, and bribe the politicians and police. Our decision on whom to help and which villages and homes to raid were not haphazardly done. We had excellent intelligence."

By 1983, Phoolan had committed numerous murders and at least 30 kidnappings, criminal activities that put a price of $10,000 on her head.

Phoolan's happiness ended when Vikram was killed by one of his own men, Sri Ram, a bandit who had been close to Babu Gujar. After Vikram's death, Phoolan was taken to a village where she was tortured and abused for three weeks until an old Brahmin took pity on her and helped her escape to the nearby jungle. A shepherd woman found her and nursed her back to health. When well enough to travel, the Bandit Queen began to plot her revenge, determined to hunt down Vikram's killer.

On February 14, 1981, she showed up with a band of dacoits at the remote village of Behmai in northern India. What followed became know as India's version of the St. Valentine's Day Massacre. The Bandit Queen believed the village was harboring Sri Ram Singh and his brother Lala Ram, and she demanded that the villagers turn them over. The villagers denied they had seen the two men, but Phoolan did not believe them.

Through a megaphone she screamed: "You are lying. I will teach you to tell the truth!"

She had 30 of the village's young men rounded up and marched them single file to a river, where they were shot. Only eight survived the massacre. It was described as the largest dacoit massacre since the founding of modern India and "so shocking to Indians because of its scale, because it was led by a woman and because women of a lower caste in India murdered men of higher standing."

Phoolan remained the most wanted criminal in India until 1983 when she and leading members of her gang surrendered. A crowed of 8,000 cheered their heroine as the authorities led her away. She spent the next 11 years in prison without trial. Meanwhile, the legend of the Bandit Queen grew when a feature film, "Bandit Queen," purportedly based on her life, was released. She disliked the movie intensely and threatened to sue its producer and director. Finally released from jail in 1994, Phoolan ran for parliament and easily won a seat, a remarkable achievement for a woman who had never learned to read or write. As a parliamentarian, Phoolan championed the rights of women and the poor and fought for an end to child marriage.

The former Bandit Queen claimed she had reformed, but she could not leave her past behind. On July 25, 2001, three masked gunmen ambushed and shot her to death outside her Delhi home. No one knows for sure who the killers were, but in death she became one of the most legendary figures in Indian history.

INDIAN WOMEN CONTINUE to pursue activism on behalf of women's rights, more in the spirit of Gandhi than the Bandit Queen. On January 30, 2009, the Gulabi Gang actively participated in the first Ahimsa Non-Violence Day in New Delhi, which was aimed at using the spirit of non violence popularized by the revered Mahatma Gandhi. When a woman was raped in the streets of Bombay in 1978, Indian women of the city organized a Reclaim the Night March.

Twenty-eight years later, in 2006 Jasmeen Patheja organized Blank Noise to emulate the Take Back the Night marches that had been organized around the world to assert the right of women to walk in public places without fear. Two police vans stood by to ensure their safety and with good reason. The following year, Mumbai experienced a mob assault on two women who had talked back to a group of men who had been harassing them. In large parts of India, especially in the rural conservative areas, women face rampant hostility and violence when they go out in public, especially after dark. The practice in India is known as "eve teasing."

Women activists in India have also initiated a pink chaldi (underwear) campaign after a group of men chased and beat up women when they left a pub on January 24, 2009. The following February, the pink chaldi campaign called for a Pub Bharo (Fill the Pubs) action campaign on St. Valentine's Day.

Delhi-based journalist Nisha Susnan, who started the campaign, wrote in her blog: "Go to a pub wherever you are. From Kabul to Chennai to Singapore to LA, women have signed up. It does not matter if you are actually not a pub goer or even much of a drinker. Let us raise a toast (it can be juice) to Indian women."

Bright gulabi (pink) chaldis were sent to one of the prominent individuals arrested in the January 24 attack.

It is not clear whether the Pink Chaldi campaign was inspired by the Gulabi Gang, but no doubt Sampat would have approved of how the Pink Chaldi took aggressive action. Sampat and her followers believe that the oppressed can not fight alone. Power can only come through struggle against the established order.

In Sampat's words: "Any woman who is struggling is with me. It's their battle and I am training them. In training them, they discover their strength and courage."

THE GULABI GANG'S campaign has brought it fame that today extends well beyond India's borders. The gang has launched a website to spread the word about its work. A French publisher learned of the Gulabi Gang and formed GULABI, a French-based organization that supports Sampat's work. The publisher has also launched a book in French about Sampat. Meanwhile, the press in France, Spain, U.S., U.K. and Canada has profiled the Gulabi Gang's work. In Helsinki, a class of college students organized a fund raising concert to aid the Gulabi Gang, while students studying women's rights have traveled to India to meet her.

Award-winning British film maker Kim Longinotto made a documentary about the Gulabi Gang that won an award as the best documentary at the Abu Dhabi Film Festival in October 2010. Longinotto said she would use the $100,000 prize money to help make the future of the girls profiled in her film better. The film features five women who came to Sampat with their concerns about child marriage and mistreatment by their husbands.

No doubt, Sampat and her gang are making a difference for women in rural India. A brave and determined woman has challenged the status quo and convinced poor women that they control their destinies, if they have the courage and band together to stand up to corrupt authority.

The lesson: Individually women are weak, but together as a group, they can be strong. The message—women have power and can control their destinies. It is a lesson and message that oppressed women around the world can surely learn and heed.

ACKNOWLEDGEMENTS

Many individuals helped make this book possible by stepping forward and generously providing their time, resources, and sage advice. First, I would like thank those who helped to provide documents and photographs for the book. They include David Gardey, Jeff Lewis and Tony Manheim. Chuck Lutz and Stephanie and Larry Vezina read and helped edit the manuscript and offered valuable suggestions on how to improve it: Charles Lutz and Stephanie and Larry Vezina. I appreciate their patience and time and being a big part of my writing career. Also, a special thanks to Charles Lutz for

sharing his law enforcement expertise and helping to make this book much more accurate than it would have been without his generous assistance. Another special thank to my wife, Magdalena, for her love and for support of my writing career. Ann Thomas of the Interlibrary Loan Department of Winthrop University in my hometown of Rock Hill, South Carolina, was invaluable in finding books, articles and microfilm and other research materials essential to the project's completion. Patti Stafford and Jackie McFadden of the Documents Department of Winthrop University were also helpful in locating U.S. government books, articles and government reports.

Thanks also to Dimas Harya, my talented business partner from Jakarta, Indonesia, whom I was lucky enough to meet on my Fulbright assignment to that country. Dimas played an important role in publishing this book. I look forward to working with him on other projects.

—Ron Chepesiuk

SELECTED BIBLIOGRAPHY

BOOKS

Adler, Polly, A House is Not a Home, Amherst, Massachusetts, University of Massachusetts Press, 1996

Burroughs, Brian, Public Enemies: America's Greatest Crime Wave and the Birth of the FBI, 1933-34, New York, Penguin, 2009

Chepesiuk, Ron, Gangsters of Harlem, Fort Lee, New Jersey, Barricade Books, 2005

------------------, Gangsters of Miami, Fort Lee, New Jersey, Barricade Books, 2009

Devi, Phoolan, and Others, The Bandit Queen India, Guilford, Connecticut, Lyons Press, 2006

Devito, Calvo, The Encyclopedia of International Organized Crime, "Maria Lucciardi (A.K.A La Piccolina), New York, Checkmark Book, 2005

Edmonds Andy, Bugsy's Baby: The Secret Life of Mob Queen Virginia Hill., New York, Carol Publishing Corporation 1993

Fianduco, Giovanni, Women and the Mafia Female: Roles in Organized Crime Structures, Springer, New York, 2003

Guinn, Jeff, Go Down Together: The True Untold Story of Bonnie and Clyde, New York, Simon and Shuster,

Hamilton, Stanley, Machine Gun Kelly's Last Stand, Lawrence, Kansas, University Press of Kansas, 2003

Longrigg, Clare, Mafia Women, London, England, Chatto and Windows, 1997

------------------, No Questions Asked: The Secret Life of Women in the Mob, New York, Miramax, 2004

Lythgoe, Gertrude, The Bahama Queen, Mystic, Connecticut, Flack Hammock Press, 2006

Milner, E.R.M., The Lives and Times of Bonnie and Clyde, Carbondale, Illinois, Southern Illinois University Press, 2005

Moran, Judith, Judith Moran: My Story, Sidney Australia, Random House Australia, 2005

Scherer Garcia, Julio, La Rena de Pacifico, Mexico City, Mexico, Grijalbo Minlahon, 2008

Shakur, Assata, Angela Davis, Assata: An Autobiography, Chicago, Lawrence Hill and Company, 2003

Siebert, Renate, Secrets Life and Death: Women and the Mafia, London, England, Verso, 1996

Sifakis, Carl, The Mafia Encyclopedia, New York, Checkmark Books, 2005

Smitten, Richard, The Godmother, New York, Pocket, 1990

Sylvester, John, and Andrew Rule, Leadbelly: The True Inside Story of an Underworld War, London, England, John Blake, 2005

Tomlinson, Gerald, Murder in New Jersey, Rutgers University Press, Chicago, Lawrence Hill and Company, 2003

MAGAZINE AND NEWSPAPER ARTICLES

Agren, David, "Female Felons Abound in Mexico," USA Today, Dec, 2010, p. 9A

"Alleged Gang Godmother, Corrupt Police on Stand," China-daily.com.cn, Oct. 15, 2009

Anderson. Paul, "Judy Moran and Three Others Charged over Desmond Moran Killing," The Herald Sun, June 16, 2009

-------------------"Judy Moran Will Stand Trial in Supreme Court for the Murder of Tuppence Moran," Herald Sun, April 10, 2010

Associated Press, "Police Coordinate Team to Stop Gang Wars in Miami," Dec. 29, 1998

---------------------, Miami Gang Leader Gets Out of Jail," June 6, 2000

Bachelard, Michael, "Slur Sees Moran Memoir Pulped. The Australian, May 29, 2005

Bell, Thomas, "Once the 'Queen' of Washington's Underworld, Odessa Madre Dies Penniless," The Washington Post, May 8, 1990, pp DC 11

"Big Time Female Drug Suspect Seizes Mexico's Imagination," The Associated Press, Oct. 5, 2007

Calvo, Oscar, "Gang Warfare Heats Up In Miami," SunSentinel, May 12, 1998

Chuanjiao, Xie, "China's Organized Crime Increases in 2008," China Daily, Feb. 2, 2009

Chung, Olivia, "Bo's Death March Towards Beijing," Asia Times, April 21, 2010

Contreras, Joe, "Underworld Queen," Newsweek, Oct. 11, 2007

Dhillon, Amrit, "Pretty In Pink, Female Vigilantes Also Handy with an Axe," The Age, December 15, 2007

------------------The Pink Sari Gang," South China Morning Post, May 19, 1993

Dunbar, Polly, "The Pink Vigilantes," Mail on Sunday (London), January 20, 2008, FB, p. 59

Ewing, Kent, "Bo Xilai: China's Brash Populist," AsiaTimes, March 19, 2010

----------------"Chinas; Brash Populist," AsiaTimes, March 19, 2010

"Female Gang in India Operates Dressed in Pink," National Public Radio, Nov., 24, 2008

Gaines-Carter, Patricia, "Heyday of the Flamingo," The Washington Post, March 5, 1989, p. D1

Grillo, Joan, "Mexico's Female Narcos," GlobalPost, December 19, 2010

"Gulabi Gang Makes Men in Khaki Run for Cover," Hindustan Times, August 18, 2006

Hewitt, Sue, "The Gang's All Here," Herald Sun, March 11, 2007

Jacobs, Andrew, "Chinese Trial Reveals Vast Web of Corruption and Fuels a Political Career," The New York Times, Section A, p.6

"Judy Moran Signs with Harry Miller," Sydney Morning Herald, April 12, 2004

Krishnan, Ananth, "China Tightens Corruption Law, The Hindu, July 12, 2010

Lyons. Rick, "Coke Queens," Sunday Star (UK), Feb. 10, 2008

Macartney, Jane, "Godmother of Chinese Gangsters, Xie Caiping, Jailed for 18 years," Timesonline, Nov. 4, 2009

Marder, Murrey, "Jury Hears Former Pink Club Operator," The Washington Post, May 25, 1948, p.1 plus

McKinley, James C., "In Mexico, A Fugitive's Arrest Captivates the Cameras," New York Times, Oct. 12, 2007

"Mexico Enthralled by Drug Queen," Mobile Register (Alabama), Oct. 5, 2007, p A14

Minihan, Mary, "The Great Mafia Mozzarrella Scandal," The Independent, March 29, 2008

"Miss Madre Arrested in Narcotics case," The Washington Post, Jan., 11, 1949, p. B1

Molloy, Courtland, "A Detective and an Underworld Queen," The Washington Post, May 27, 1990, p. B3 A

----------------------, "The Odessa Files: The Life and Times of the Queen of "Washington's Underworld," The Washington Post, May 7, 2010

Montalbano, William D., "Mafia Arrest in Italy Nets Female Boss," Los Angeles Times, Feb. 9, 1993

--------------------------, 'Top Fugitives Arrest Deals a Blow to Mafia," Los Angeles Times, May 19, 1993

Murphy, Padraic, and Anthony Dowsley, "Underworld Matriarch Allegedly Loses Turf War," Herald Sun, January 9, 2010

Olson, Alexandra, "Mexican Judge Absolves Reputed Drug Cartel Queen," Associated Press, Dec. 3, 2010

"Once Queen of Underworld Gets 10 years in Narcotics Case," The Washington Post, Jan. 27 1962, p. C4

Paull, Joseph, Women Underworld Figure is heard by.DC Rackets Jury," The Washington Post, Feb. 12, 1962, p. B1

"Pink Gang Uses Tough Tactics against Misbehaving Males," The Irish Times, Dec. 5, 2007

"Pink Vigilantes Take Aim at Rural Justice," South China Morning Post, February 15, 2009

Prasad, Raekha, "Banda Sisters," The Guardian, Feb. 15, 2008

"Prison Boss Sacked after Alleged Trafficker Gets Botox in Jail," The Guardian (London) Dec. 3, 2011

Roberts, Greg, "Judy Moran says Barbara Williams Makes her Hair Stand on End," The Daily Telegraph April 23, 2009

Roy, Nilanjana S., "Fearlessly, Speaking Out to Stop Abuse; The Female Factor," The International Herald Tribune, Aug. 4, 2010, p. 2

Rout, Milanda, "Judy Moran Expected to Make Bail Application after House Fire Set," The Australian, June 17, 2009

Rout, Milanda, and Lauren Wilson, "Judy Moran Denied Bail Over Gun Bust,' The Australian, June 18, 2009

Shengxia, Song, 'Godmother of Chongqing Crime Gang Sentenced to 18 Years," Global Times, November 24, 2009

Simpson, John, Taking on Corruption in Booming China," BBC.com, April 7, 2010

Smith, J. Y., "Vice Queen Arrested in Gaming Raid," The Washington Post, Oct. 13, 1973, p. B1

Stevenson, Mark, "Accused Female Drug Lord Ordered Held Over for Trial in Mexico," Associated Press, Oct. 5, 2007

"Suspicious Blaze at Judy; Moran's House, ABC News, June 17, 2009

"Take No Guff a Source of Inspiration," Canwest News Service, October 6, 2010

"The Red and the Black," The Economist, Oct. 1, 2009

Think Pink," Indian Express, Sept. 14, 2010

Topsfield, Jewel, and Adam Morton, "Underworld M an Shot in Broad Daylight," The Sydney Morning Telegraph, June 22, 2003

Tuckman. Jo, "Easy Money, Heavy Price; Woman Join Mexico's Drug Wars," The Guardian (London), Dec. 6, 2010, p. 198

----------------, "Mexican Police Capture the Queen of Drug Trafficking," The Observer (England) Sept., 30, 3007 p. 40

INTERNET SOURCES

Amoruso, David, Maria "La Piccolina" Licciardi", Gangsters Incorporated. http://gangstersinc.com

"Big Anti-Mafia Sweep Under way in Italy, U.S.," Canada.com

Bruno, Anthony, Phoolan Devi: The Bandit Queen of India, www.trutv.com

Diaz-Duran, Constantino, "Queenpins of the Drug Cartels," www.thedailybeast.com/blogs

"Gangland Widow Moran Fails to Win Bail," http://www.stuff.co.nz

"Washington DC," http//www.lonelyplanet.com/usa/Washing-ton-dc/history

PRIMARY DOCUMENTS

Miami Dade Police, Memorandum, "Homicide Task Force," 2000 to 2003, 2010

United States. v. Avonda Dowling, David Gardey, Opening Statement

United State v. Avonda Vanay Dowling, In the United States Court of Appeals for the Eleventh Circuit, No. 04-10464, Appeal from the United States District Court for the Southern District of Florida, March 23, 2005

ABOUT THE AUTHOR

RON CHEPESIUK is award winning freelance investigative journalist and documentary producer and the host of the Crime Beat radio show. He is a Fulbright scholar and a consultant to the History Channel's Gangland documentary series. His true crime books include "Drug Lords, Black Gangsters of Chicago, Gangsters of Harlem Gangsters of Miami" and Sergeant Smack: The Lives and Times of Ike Atkinson. Kingpin, and his Band of Brothers.